Liaison
Interpr

Liaison Interpreting

A Handbook

Adolfo Gentile, Uldis Ozolins and
Mary Vasilakakos
*with Leong Ko and
Ton-That Quynh-Du*

MELBOURNE UNIVERSITY PRESS
1996

Melbourne University Press
PO Box 278, Carlton South, Victoria 3053, Australia

First published 1996

Text © Melbourne University Press 1996
Design and typography © Melbourne University Press 1996

This book is copyright. Apart from any use permitted under the *Copyright Act 1968* and subsequent amendments, no part may be reproduced, stored in a retrieval system or transmitted by any means or process whatsoever without the prior written permission of the publisher.

Designed and typeset by Jan Schmoeger/Designpoint,
in 10.5/14 Berthold Baskerville Book
Printed in Malaysia by SRM Production Services Sdn. Bhd.

National Library of Australia Cataloguing-in-Publication data

Gentile, Adolfo.
  Liaison interpreting: a handbook.

  Bibliography.
  Includes index.
  ISBN 0 522 84581 9.

  1. Translating and interpreting. I. Ozolins, Uldis, 1948– .
  II. Vasilakakos, Mary. III. Title.

418.02

*To George Strauss,
one of the founders of
interpreting/translating
education in Australia*

Contents

Preface	ix
Introduction	1
1 Historical Background	5
2 General Considerations	17
3 The Role of the Interpreter	30
4 The Interpreted Interview	41
5 Ethics	56
6 Professional Socialization	64

SPECIALIST AREAS OF WORK

7 Mental Health	79
8 Legal Settings *by Ton-That Quynh-Du*	89
9 Business Settings *by Leong Ko*	116
10 Speech Pathology	125
Bibliography	136
Index	142

Preface

This handbook is a collaborative effort of the staff teaching the Interpreting and Translating courses in the School of Languages, Interpreting and Translating at Deakin University. It fills a need created by the growth of liaison interpreting in non-conference settings around the world. It addresses fundamental issues of skills, techniques, role, dynamics, ethics and professionalization, as well as the particular needs of a number of specialist areas. While the experience of the authors has come largely from the Australian context, the book is intended to be useful world-wide to trainers of interpreters, students, practitioners, professionals working with interpreters, and indeed anyone who needs information about this interpreting domain.

We wish to thank our colleagues at Deakin for their encouragement and co-operation, particularly Ahmet Ozirmak and Said Shahat for their contribution to earlier drafts of the manuscript, and Ton-That Quynh-Du and Leong Ko for their contributions respectively of Chapter 8, Legal Settings and Chapter 9, Business Settings. We also thank Klaus Hermes and Leticia Worley for their many helpful suggestions.

A.G., U.O., M.V.

Introduction

This handbook is the first to tackle comprehensively the role, function and practice of liaison interpreting, and the many issues of technique, ethics and related matters met in the field.

We use the term 'liaison interpreting' to refer to a growing area of interpreting throughout the world: in business settings, where executives from different cultures and languages meet each other; in meetings between a society's legal, medical, educational and welfare institutions and its immigrants who speak a different language; in relations between a dominant society and indigenous peoples speaking different languages; in a whole host of less formal situations in tourism, education and cultural contacts.

Liaison interpreting is the style adopted in these varied settings—a style where the interpreter is physically present in an interview or meeting, and usually uses the consecutive mode of interpreting. This field of interpreting has grown immensely in recent decades, at some remove from the already established field of international conference interpreting whose practitioners work mainly in the simultaneous mode, often quite anonymously to their listeners.

The need for this handbook has two sources. For a start, while considerable attention has been paid in the past to training and research issues related to simultaneous interpreting, a literature on issues of liaison interpreting has emerged only very slowly and in a more scattered way. Secondly, the field of liaison interpreting has suffered from serious problems of status and understanding on the part of those most vitally affected by it—the users. While delegations at international conferences take it for granted that their meetings are catered for by interpreters, those who work with liaison interpreters are often unsure as to respective roles and expectations or to questions of technique and ethics.

In most countries where immigrant or indigenous populations who speak other languages have encounters with mainstream institutions and professionals in such areas as welfare, health or the law, there have been quite *ad hoc* approaches to interpreting. Other family members may interpret, clients may bring an interpreter, or untrained casual interpreters may be used. Such practices enforce the view that interpreting needs can be dealt with in a makeshift manner. Often the quality of the interpreting is highly variable, often the 'interpreters' assume roles completely outside those necessary to interpret and, all too often, negative attitudes towards minority groups are transferred to interpreters from those groups. Thus, interpreters have often been seen as advocates for minorities, rather than as increasing the efficiency of the host institutions. Ironically, a similar issue of status arises in the eyes of established international conference interpreters, who have often seen liaison interpreting as being essentially different to their own work; only in very recent years have conference interpreters played a part in developing liaison interpreting.

More positively, we can now point to an emerging appreciation across the world of liaison interpreting needs. First, *ad hoc* approaches are giving way to a serious concern to ensure quality interpreting. In some cases, this has been in specific areas of constitutional guarantees or other legislative requirements (e.g. federal laws relating to legal interpreting in the United States), at other times to more comprehensive schemes of accreditation and training of interpreters and education of personnel who work with interpreters (as in Australia and some Scandinavian countries). Secondly, the complexity of this field is now being appreciated by key people and institutions in business, law, medicine or wherever, so that interpreting is seen as enabling them to fulfil their particular objectives. Attitudes are shifting away from a suspicious view of interpreters as a nuisance or at best a necessary evil, and towards recognition of interpreting as a professional area of expertise.

As a result, we see now in various parts of the world concerns with such issues as accreditation, training, registration, quality control, ethical issues and industrial matters. In fact, these issues are no less clear-cut and no less capable of being articulated than in the established field of international conference interpreting.

The book begins with a historical account of interpreting, looking at the various situations around the world where multilingual populations have needed ways of communicating. It looks at the development of liaison interpreting in the context of increased population movement and multinational contact in the decades since World War II, and then presents a considered view of what the role and performance of a liaison interpreter should be and an account of the standard settings for interpreting.

World-wide, liaison interpreters work in situations that vary greatly in terms of understanding of their role, relations with their co-workers and clients, and degree of performance expected of them. Despite this diversity, guidelines can be clearly enunciated for what a professional performance of liaison interpreting involves, what role, techniques and ethics the interpreter must adopt, and what outcomes the interpreter is and is not responsible for. This discussion is grounded in examples drawn from practice, and from the theoretical literature.

We then look at some areas that present peculiar issues for liaison interpreters, either because of settings that demand particular roles or place restrictions (business settings, court-rooms), or because of the status that communication itself plays in proceedings (mental health, much legal interaction, and speech pathology). Often, parties are not so much interested in communication in terms of the delivery of 'normal' messages, but may be interested in language for forensic or diagnostic or intelligence purposes; in mental health, treatment itself may be through communicative therapies. The status of language here presents particular issues for liaison interpreters that might be quite unknown to the conference interpreter. Such interpreting may also be carried out in situations of great stress, conflict, confusion or emotion, and we consider these areas to present some of the greatest challenges to liaison interpreting. While legal interpreting has gained a deal of attention in recent years, the other areas we examine have not, though the challenges they raise are just as great.

This handbook is intended in the first instance for those training as interpreters in the many training institutions around the world. While the contributors have largely gained their experience of interpreting in Australia, this book is not restricted to issues of practice in any one country. Most of the issues that interpreters have to confront, such as those of technique, ethics and role, are common across all countries where liaison interpreting is establishing itself.

Secondly, it is intended for the many practising interpreters where systems of training or accreditation have not yet developed. In many countries, liaison interpreters have to carve out their own practice in an often uncomprehending environment, and establish professional standards where interpreting has not ever been thought of as a professional activity.

Finally, we feel it will also be of use to the many people in different walks of life who regularly need to work with interpreters: business people wondering how to gain understanding of negotiations with overseas companies; lawyers, judges, magistrates or police interested in issues of legal interpreting; employees in various situations who feel that inadequate language services hamper their work; clients who feel that lack of interpreters makes it difficult for them to receive adequate consideration from various institutions they encounter and, not least, civil servants and parliamentarians whose actions or decisions can affect all areas of liaison interpreting.

The book is a pioneer, and our hope is that it will make the work of liaison interpreters more understandable both to those they work with and to the interpreters themselves.

1 Historical Background

The diversity of languages has, throughout history, created the need for methods of communication between speakers of different languages. Interpreting—the oral transfer of messages between speakers of different languages—is thus one of the oldest of human activities, and the role of the interpreter is arguably one of the oldest of the professions.

However, *multilingual situations do not always require interpreting*. For some groups, individual and group multilingualism is a common feature: individuals growing up in close proximity to other language groups often develop the capacity to speak a number of languages. Examples include the notable multilingualism of Australian Aboriginal groups, of many small Middle Eastern groups from antiquity and, more generally, borderland regions throughout the world. In this context, the practice of interpreting is rare.

In other situations, communication problems may be overcome by use of a recognized lingua franca, generally not the mother tongue. Latin, Arabic and many other languages have at times gained this status, often within certain domains (e.g. religion, education, trade). The evolution of French as a diplomatic language from the sixteenth to twentieth centuries is a specific example, to which we will return.

In some situations, certain social groups gain multilingual skills because of their particular social roles. Thus traders (who in some older societies had a marginal or even pariah status) play the part of intermediaries, either through a command of a lingua franca or through developed multilingualism, to further their trading and social contacts. A relatively small number of multilinguals are entrusted (or tolerated) to communicate with others, in a setting where such contacts with speakers of other languages tend to be limited, and limited to specific domains.

Where geographical boundaries are sharp, there may have been little understanding of the language of others who lived even a little distance away. If contact was relatively restricted, this situation may have existed for centuries. While this can lead to social antagonism and even conflicts, in many cases a perfectly harmonious relationship can endure, with neither group feeling either antipathy or interest in the other.

In the above four situations, populations with different languages can live side by side, without the widespread use of interpreting. Indeed, for much of antiquity and even modern history, an identifiable role of interpreting was usually seen only in certain settings—often related to international contacts at the highest level, such as courtly visits, delegations to other countries, or intrepid explorers; or as a facet of the general spread of colonialism throughout the world. The status of the 'interpreter' varied greatly. At one extreme, the interpreter might be a highly educated and trusted official who would interpret when his ruler met another ruler. Until the very last century such meetings were in fact rare; far more common was the use of ambassadors or plenipotentiaries who were linguistically equipped for service in other countries at international meetings. On the other hand, the linguistic go-between might be a lowly slave or 'native' who learnt the language of the colonizers and served them in colonialist expansion, or a priest who had made a study of another language to help the task of religious proselytization.

Interpreting as a recognized and distinct area of expertise, and certainly as a particular social role, arrived only with modernity, and as a result of the curious new ways in which individuals and populations speaking different languages have had to interact.

1 HISTORICAL BACKGROUND

The place of *translation* has always been important. Many of the most crucial texts in a society (e.g. religious texts) come from other languages, necessitating generations of professional translators, usually church officials or scholars. Yet while this function of rendering texts into other languages is quite old and is generally well recognized, the modern role of the interpreter has brought a profound innovation to international contacts.

Conference interpreting

The first distinct interpreting role to be recognized was that of the international conference interpreter—a very recent development.

In previous centuries, French had gained ascendancy as the international language of diplomacy, and all who engaged in international affairs until the early twentieth century could use French. As a symbolic crowning of this dominance, at the Congress of Vienna in 1815, where the powers of Europe sought to punish and limit the ambitions of post-Napoleonic France and where the concern was to roll back France's hitherto empire and assert the strength of other European powers, the language used for official proceedings was—French.

A number of studies have identified the Versailles peace talks in 1918–19 as the beginning of modern international interpreting: significantly, the leaders of two great powers—Britain and the United States—who attended the peace talks did not speak French (Herbert, 1978; Roland, 1892). Armed forces in Europe had increasingly had to deal with the various languages of their allies or enemies, and always had officers with a good command of languages for such liaison; now, some of these military officers were hastily conscripted to fill the role of interpreters at Versailles, performing consecutive interpreting for large gatherings or liaison interpreting in more intimate meetings. These experiments developed further with the general rise of international contacts after World War I and, while military officers continued to serve as interpreters at the very top levels, civilian interpreters also gained work in organizations such as the League of Nations. While struggling to develop a suitable technique, and always mindful particularly of the difficulties of consecutive interpreting, these innovations did establish for interpreters a permanent place at international gatherings.

A significant advance for conference interpreters came immediately after World War II when, at the Nuremberg war crimes trials, new technology allowed experiments with simultaneous interpreting, whereby interpreters worked from sound-proof booths and relayed their messages through earphones to the listeners in the court-room. This methodology was quickly adopted at most international meetings, particularly the United Nations and its many organizations, and laid the basis for the very rapid development of an international conference interpreting profession. Civilians now quickly outnumbered military personnel, and they established their own body—the International Association of Conference Interpreters (AIIC)—which acted as a professional organization, an industrial body and to some extent a closed shop in the post-war decades, ensuring high standards and good remuneration for its members. Where the interpreting was simultaneous, interpreters generally worked into their strongest language only, but often from two or more other languages. Despite the high profile of simultaneous interpreting, consecutive interpreting was still often used in smaller meetings or where deliberations could be slower, such as in the Security Council of the United Nations. Interpreting schools slowly developed to train future interpreters, again maintaining strict standards and accepting only the cream of candidates.

International conference interpreting gained its status from its milieu and its clientele. The interpreters tended to come from the same restricted social background as the politicians and diplomats and government officials they interpreted for, and had generally gained their linguistic skills from residence or study in a number of countries. This was a strongly Eurocentric and conservative professional caste, with a virtual monopoly on international conference interpreting.

Liaison interpreting

Liaison interpreting grew up in quite different circumstances. It has not always been seen by conference interpreters as an area of

1 HISTORICAL BACKGROUND

interpreting in its own right, but rather as a residual arm of language work at best, or multilingual welfare work (often with a charity air) at worst.

In the post-World War II decades, several social and economic developments led to its growth. The two main areas of development were in international business contacts (where conference interpreters did at times have some input) and, less spectacularly but more pervasively, in relation to immigrant and indigenous populations who did not speak the dominant language of their society. The massive growth of immigration in the post-war world, affecting not only traditional immigration countries such as the Americas but increasingly all nations, has been the greatest spur to the growth of liaison interpreting. No less socially important has been the continuing hard-fought battle for recognition of the needs and rights of indigenous peoples, in societies that had often paid them little attention.

To an extent, the spread of *international business contacts* has extended the range of work of conference interpreters, who have generally seen a continuum between their work in official international conferences and organizations, and in private business meetings and negotiations. However, in the interpreting that now is commonplace between mainstream institutions and immigrant or indigenous populations, there has been less involvement by conference interpreters.

The lines of development of liaison interpreting for *immigrant and indigenous populations* have been remarkably similar throughout the world, though often with notable differences in terms of rate of development, focus of attention, political and social context and recognition of the processes. Interpreting has been a generally *ad hoc* response to the needs either of the minority language populations or of mainstream institutions.

In a variety of settings, native administrators, agriculturalists, welfare workers and others have established contact with indigenous populations, almost invariably using members of the indigenous group to interpret. When there are sufficient numbers of migrants, there will be individuals (again usually from the minority group)

9

who emerge to interpret either on a voluntary basis or as hired would-be professionals. At this stage, the activity of interpreting is more widespread than the role of the interpreter. Often family or friends or casual contacts who are to some extent bilingual are used to interpret messages. Consciousness of the role of the interpreter is limited and generally of little interest either to the minority group or to institutions that often see interpreting as a necessary evil. One significant consequence has been the poor remuneration and industrial status, neglected professional development, and inadequate management and policy direction experienced by those wanting to work professionally as liaison interpreters.

In situations where it becomes clear that the need for interpreting is more or less permanent, and has consequences for the minority group and mainstream social institutions, organized responses of various kinds are experimented with to ensure some minimum of standards (sometimes for fear of legal repercussions) and reliability. In some counties, such interpreting is organized along private lines, with minimal outside accreditation, setting of standards or supervision. In other cases, governments focus on certain areas, usually the legal system (for example, the need to meet constitutional guarantees for non-English speakers in the United States) and quite exacting accreditation standards can be demanded. In a few cases (for example, Australia and some Scandinavian countries), there are more comprehensive controls over standards and accreditation to meet general interpreting needs, as well as attention to related issues such as training.

Liaison interpreters in such settings have generally not achieved the same degree of professional organization and control as have conference interpreters, even though the nature of the work and the skills necessary may be equally demanding, and form a continuum of professional endeavour rather than distinct activities.

A related question, now increasingly being asked around the world, concerns the degree of official interest and intervention necessary in relation to liaison interpreting needs. Interpreting provision tends to follow (at some distance) more general orientations towards welfare of indigenous or immigrant populations. In the case of Germany, for example, where the status of immigrants is often that of a guest-worker and there is considerable politicization of the extent of state responsibility towards these groups, official government involvement in provision or monitoring of interpreters tends to be patchy and restricted to narrow fields (for example, the legal system). Many non-German speaking immigrants find an often unspoken onus on *them* to provide an interpreter if, say, they see a doctor or an official in a public bureaucracy. In other countries, Australia being an example, public provision is made across a whole range of institutions to ensure communication with non-English speakers. The rationale is that immigration is for permanent settlement, and that the government has a responsibility to provide the means for satisfactory settlement of all immigrants.

Differences in role and status

Just as international conference interpreters gain their status from the reflected status of the clients they serve, so do liaison interpreters in their varied work settings. The question of status and reflected status in turn profoundly influences how their role and contribution are understood: prevailing social and institutional norms will strongly affect the way in which the interpreter's function is understood.

In relation to international business contacts, while to some extent this field has developed out of the model of international diplomatic interpreting, in many cases the use of interpreters has only developed with the burgeoning of substantial international trade since the 1960s. Many businesses around the world will, before using professional interpreters, choose a variety of other means of bridging the language gap. Common practices are the use of agents who speak appropriate languages, the use of in-house staff members with no professional background in interpreting, or reliance on the other party's interpreters. There has been a gradual developmental and consciousness-raising process as increasing numbers of chief executives or other significant personnel wish to engage in direct communication with their business opposites, in which case interpreting is a necessity. Significantly, awareness of the need for interpreting and, more generally, for businesses to be prepared to work with other languages, has often been lacking in many companies which speak a major language such as English. Complaints about the unwillingness of American or British companies to recognize the necessity for other languages have often been raised (Simon, 1980).

The practice of business interpreting often shades off into other activities that reflect the protean nature of business contacts and the lack of clarity between interpreting and other roles—such as tourism interpreting and guide-work, which is more often monolingual or bilingual work linked to other roles. At the other end, business interpreting covers the full ceremonial paraphernalia of business visits including entertaining, intelligence-gathering and other activities that perhaps fall outside the role of the interpreter strictly defined but seem a necessary concomitant of business interpreting. These issues will be raised again in Chapters 3 and 9.

We do not intend to convey an impression of conference interpreting as an untroubled example of professional achievement, and liaison interpreting as an unco-ordinated and barely appreciated area of confusion. International conference interpreting needs now to confront a series of challenges—particularly the diversity of languages now being used in international conferences, and the diversity of practitioners—which give rise to some of the policy and professional issues well-known to liaison interpreting. And for liaison interpreting, despite the diversity of current practice, a clearly definable logic unites the field. Where there is a need to communicate across language barriers in social settings of business, immigrant or indigenous populations, increasingly there is official and professional awareness of the need to provide services.

Bilingual aides, bilinguals, do-gooders and other non-interpreters

We have identified differences in status as being crucial in understanding the ready professional acceptance of conference interpreters, and the greater opacity of the role and function of the liaison interpreter. Only a clear understanding of the status of the social activities in which the liaison interpreter is engaged will enable us to accurately predict how the role will be understood. A generally low valuing of the need to communicate with speakers of other languages (the guest-worker situation, or racist response to immigration or indigenous groups) will be reflected in the social evaluation of the interpreter's role.

Often in the past (and still sometimes in the present), interpreting has been carried out by people with some bilingual skills who have been willing, or who have social obligations, to help those unable to speak the dominant language. Thus, for example, those who have developed skills in the dominant language more quickly (for example, older resident immigrants from the same background, or children of recent arrivals), interpret for their family, friends or the immigrant community generally. Indeed, the almost ubiquitous use of family or friends, and the presumption that this is an adequate means of solving the language gap, seems to be a virtually unavoidable phase in the development of interpreting in these settings. It is not difficult to understand the horror of professional interpreters or most professional service providers at such practices. But in situations where such communication is evaluated as a lowly activity, this is often the most common form of interpreting, and regarded as a quite acceptable practice in institutions. Especially where non-speakers of the dominant language are socially isolated, or confronted by negative attitudes, the provision of such help may be all that is available.

The participation of large numbers of bilinguals as interpreters generally has a lasting impact on how the role of the interpreter is seen. A presumption that service provided by relatives or friends (or perhaps a casual other, such as a hospital worker from a minority group) is adequate, places the onus on the non-speaker of the dominant language to provide such a 'helper'. It is then a short step to seeing any interpreter performing that role as 'helping' the immigrant or indigenous person. In almost all cases, the interpreter comes from the same background, for few of the dominant group will know the minority language (which will often have low social status). Thus, the ethnicity or speech community membership of the interpreter is another significant factor in how the interpreter is accepted.

Such bilingual 'help' is often the antithesis of interpreting. While in some situations it may allow some understanding between the parties, the broader impact upon roles and status can be devastating. Moreover, uncontrolled use of helpers can lead to serious miscommunication or worse: children being used as interpreters in some crucial settings is clearly inappropriate, cruel and even dangerous. It is only slowly being recognized that the use of such 'helpers' represents a serious breach of ethics on the part of the professional, official or worker from any institution that has to deal with speakers of a minority language.

A variety of other roles and functions performed by bilinguals must be carefully defined in contradistinction to interpreting.

Bilingual aides have a capacity in two or more languages and use another language in the direct conduct of their primary role (for example, an airline booking clerk, a social welfare officer etc.). They can conduct interviews with clients in another language, keep records in the dominant language, etc. These roles do not involve transfer of message from the speaker of one language to the speaker of another language, but rather monolingual work in another language. In some multilingual countries, the ability to work in this manner in another language has long been a requirement of employment in certain capacities; in other countries, these skills are now being recognized as separate from interpreting, and supported and accredited as such.

Bilingual guides are a specific kind of bilingual aide commonly met in tourism, business travel, cultural and recreational pursuits. The expectation that an interpreter will also on many occasions be a bilingual guide is very strong. For those employing interpreters, such distinctions are often unclear, leading to an expectation that an interpreter will be a kind of bilingual dog's body, able to do many things in addition to interpreting. The danger is that these expectations intrude into the way employers or others perceive the interpreter on occasions when they are indeed functioning as interpreters: expecting, for example, the interpreter to elicit information, provide summing up, smooth over difficulties, gather intelligence etc. Equally, many employers believe that any bilingual guide can and should do interpreting. These issues are discussed further in Chapter 3.

The concept of a 'bilingual helper' is very common in pre-professional understanding of interpreting, and signals a lack of clarity in understanding the purposes of interpreting. This confusion particularly arises when there is little official recognition of language needs, and minority language groups must themselves begin the long task of lobbying for recognition of needs. For example, where a welfare rights approach is made to minority groups, 'self-help' is often the first avenue. Interpreters and often welfare and community workers, legal advisers etc. rise from the group itself, working *ad hoc* and not meeting professional criteria of accreditation or training or performance. In these circumstances, mainstream professionals will also develop innovative and not always professionally recognized routines and roles for themselves.

The ability of such groups over time to gain professional standards and a hearing from official institutions has been shown on many occasions, but the genesis of such organization is likely to blur otherwise clearly understood professional roles. Because bilingual helpers are almost always from the minority group, and virtually everyone associated with that group is an advocate of that group in official eyes, they are seen as advocates rather than as interpreters. Some helpers may indeed see themselves as bilingual advocates, and have an unclear understanding of the distinction between roles.

In summary, the development of liaison interpreting has been subject to two very influential forces that continue to determine its status and the understanding of its role. From a professional point of view, it has grown up relatively independently of, but in the shadow of, international conference interpreting. While some of the more rigid barriers are being broken down, as yet only a few conference interpreters have participated in the development of liaison interpreting, and there is still a yawning gap in terms of remuneration, social image and professional status, despite the equally demanding skills involved. Secondly, the whole field of liaison interpreting has been profoundly influenced by its own social setting of minority/majority relationships, identification with minorities and minority interests, and broader status issues.

This historical setting has produced many understandable but unnecessary obstacles in the way of accepting liaison interpreting as a distinct and appropriate professional activity. Moreover, interpreters have to battle against both their identification with the minority, and more general misunderstandings of bilingualism and the difference between speaking two languages and performing the role of interpreter.

At the heart of the matter is the constant identification of the need for interpreting with the status of the minority: *They* can't be understood; *They* don't speak our language; How can we deal with *Them* in the least time-consuming way. A change in perspective can only come when it is recognized that interpreting is not done *for* the minority group but is necessary for the successful performance of any institution that deals with clients, or any professional with clients who do not share their language. It is *as* important for institutions of the mainstream as for the minority member.

Until such an understanding is reached, liaison interpreting will continue to be identified with the minority, and views of liaison interpreting will continue to be determined by the broader social, historical and economic factors that determine relations between particular minorities and majorities.

2 General Considerations

Definitions and settings

Liaison interpreting is the name given to the genre of interpreting where the interpreting is performed in two language directions by the same person. This activity has acquired a number of epithets according to the environment within which it developed and to political considerations in the parts of the world where it is practised. In the United Kingdom, for example, this form of interpreting is called 'ad hoc' or 'public service' interpreting, in Scandinavia 'contact interpreting' and in Australia 'three-cornered' or 'dialogue' interpreting; the term 'community interpreting' is also used by a number of authors. The term 'liaison interpreting' was coined to distinguish it from 'conference interpreting' in order to circumscribe the former in an era when conference interpreters were developing a professional ethos, and to classify the sphere of operation of liaison interpreters as being of lesser importance.

While at a certain point the difference between liaison interpreting and conference interpreting becomes blurred, the situations described in this book will not be in this category.

Liaison interpreting is widely used where two or more interlocutors do not share a language and where the interpreter must be present in order to bridge the communication gap. Typically these are situations where the acquiring or giving of information is based

17

on exchanges between interlocutors which produce a resolution of some problem or lead to a decision, a diagnosis or generally improved understanding between interlocutors. These interlocutors are *ipso facto* the clients of the interpreter. Situations where these conditions obtain are many and varied, as these few examples indicate: medical consultations, teacher/parent interviews, court cases, business negotiations, group therapy, pre-trial briefings, police interviews and many more. This form of interpreting encompasses interpreting for the hearing impaired.

Factors which distinguish liaison interpreting from conference interpreting are:

- the physical proximity of interpreter and clients;
- an information gap between the clients;
- a likely status differential between the clients;
- the necessity to interpret into both language directions;
- working as an individual and not as part of a team.

Consideration of *spatial arrangements* is important for the effective and efficient performance of the interpreting function. An ideal seating pattern is where all three parties can keep eye-contact with each other; the interpreter must also be in a position which will facilitate the interpreting and will not lead either client to infer or suspect that the interpreter is taking sides. Both clients speak directly to each other rather than to the interpreter.

A triangular arrangement of seating is the optimum configuration. It is conducive to recognition of the clients as the protagonists in the situation, and leaves the interpreter to perform while allowing the clients to fully engage in the situation. The communication dynamics resemble as closely as possible those when an interpreter is not required, making it more difficult for the clients to relinquish their natural role in the communication.

This is the ideal situation, but because of the different *physical environments* in which liaison interpreting takes place, these principles must often be adapted. Familiarity with each type of environment is essential if the interpreter is to provide an optimum service.

In a clinic, for example, it is likely that only the doctor, the patient and the interpreter will be present. The environment is quiet, clean and comfortable. With minimal interference, the interpreter can concentrate and perform well. In the conference hall of a primary school, often the venue for parent/teacher interviews, many interviews are conducted at the same time, people are moving around, little children are playing and crying. The interpreter may be interrupted by the convenor for another appointment. All of this will have a bearing on the performance of the interpreter. Occasionally, as in a rehabilitation centre, the exchanges will take place in a swimming pool as requested by the physiotherapist for the purposes of treatment; the interpreter has to don a bathing suit and work in the pool.

The physical environments can vary greatly and they play an important role in effective interpreting. The interpreter must be able to adapt, concentrate and work at a satisfactory level. If the environment is such as to affect satisfactory performance, the interpreter will have to make a request for a change of location or time.

Cultural factors

Cultural factors operate at at least three levels: cultural inheritance, life experience and relative status. People who require the services of an interpreter belong by definition to different cultures in the anthropological sense—their *cultural inheritance* differs. They have been brought up in different environments with different views of the world; they have certain values and beliefs and their behaviour is influenced by these. They also have different expectations of certain situations and bring to their relationships certain assumptions about appropriate behaviour by them and others in the performance of certain tasks. In short, they have expectations, implicit assumptions and observable behaviours which differ.

Clients also differ in behaviour and assumptions due to differences in *life experiences*. Typically, in a conference interpreting situation, the people coming together have certain shared experiences due to their belonging to the same profession. For example, a group of engineers meeting annually to discuss international standards for the classification of buildings in areas prone to seismic phenomena share similar levels of education, work experience and ethos, and motivation. The language and register they use with each other will often be the product of their similar training or of reading professional journals. They will also be aware of the antecedents to the conference and of the relative status of the speakers. They can be said to be 'on the same wavelength'.

In contrast, the situations where liaison interpreting is typically carried out are at the opposite extreme. The status differential of the interlocutors will in some cases be marked, the shared experiences will be minimal and the meeting will be dictated by external factors. It may be voluntary, as would be an interview to discuss a contract for the purchase of a house, or unwanted, as in a police interview.

The interpreter must deal with both levels of cultural differences in order to properly carry out the interpreting function. Cultural knowledge is required for efficient and speedy understanding of the messages being conveyed, and to anticipate any possible sources of misunderstanding in the total exchange. The interpreter must be conversant with the elements which characterize and govern behaviour in both the cultures, and well aware of the risk of falling into facile generalizations about individuals.

These differences need to be properly addressed at the level of the interview so that any misunderstanding, embarrassment or even offence can be avoided. For instance, in certain cultures there are strong taboos regarding the exposure of one's body. In a medical situation where a woman is the patient, a male interpreter may need to decline the assignment or change the techniques used. Political refugees or victims of torture may distrust anyone from that particular cultural background or may be extremely circumspect about any authority figure. The interpreter has to call upon unusual levels of sensitivity and patience, and special arrangements may be needed so that the communication problems are not, in fact, exacerbated.

A third level of cultural factors relates to the *status differential* of the two interlocutors and the attitudes of the clients towards the interpreter. Often one of the languages is that of power and authority in the country (and is more often the language of the client wielding power and authority) and the other is the language of a minority group—and often a language of 'limited diffusion' in that country even though it may be one of the main world languages. This considerable difference in the status of the two interlocutors is not so much inherent as due to the fact that one is in an inferior social position with respect to the dominant culture of the country. In addition, the interpreter is likely to belong to the same ethnic group as the client speaking the 'lower status' language. These dynamics impinge directly on the interpreter.

Each client makes certain assumptions which place the interpreter in a difficult ethical position *vis-à-vis* the professional standards of interpreting. There is overt identification with the interpreter by the client speaking the 'lower status' language, and assumptions are made by the speaker of the hegemonic language about the interpreter being the instrument of the dominant culture. Both clients expect the interpreter to behave in a fashion that recognizes their own standpoint. In practical terms, utterances and actions which are clearly beyond the content of the communication at hand are addressed directly to the interpreter. Asides such as 'this person won't take no for an answer' and 'the system is biased against us' addressed to the interpreter cause considerable difficulty and are not conducive to a professional outcome from the interpreter's point of view. These asides often degenerate to requests of an opinion from the interpreter about matters and events being discussed. See Chapter 5 on ethics.

Cultural aspects play a decisive role in the performance of the interpreting function. The cultural dimension is intertwined and often inseparable from questions of interpreting technique; this is especially evident in the interpreter's preparation for an assignment. The briefing from both clients about the subject matter of the interview needs to be handled extremely carefully to avoid either client assuming, during the interview, that the interpretation will be supplemented with what was discussed at the briefing. This vitiates the very essence of the interpreter's function and produces some practical problems during the interview itself which destroy the notion of exchanges between interlocutors with the interpreter as a facilitator of communication. The interpreter must decide on the best method for obtaining a briefing prior to the assignment without going into too much detail with the clients. This may be to obtain as much information as possible when the booking is made and to avoid waiting in the company of one client before the assignment.

Modes of interpreting

Liaison interpreting and conference interpreting are *types* or genres of interpreting. There are two basic *modes* in which interpreting is performed, the first being *consecutive* interpreting and the second, *simultaneous*. Each mode has at least two variants, which are used in liaison interpreting.

Essentially, consecutive interpreting entails waiting for the speaker to complete a speech or a segment thereof before the interpreting begins, and simultaneous interpreting entails starting the interpretation soon after the speaker begins and continuing until just after the speaker has finished. The accepted international practice for conference interpreting has the interpreter generally going only into the 'mother' tongue in both modes of interpreting. This practice is not followed in liaison interpreting.

A distinction is made between consecutive interpreting in 'conference settings' and in 'liaison settings'. But the boundaries are not rigid or finite and the essential element which distinguishes these settings is that in one case the interpreter works into one language only and in the other works both into and out of one language.

Consecutive interpreting in 'conference settings' is employed where audience interaction is required as is typically the case in conference workshops, working groups, syndicate groups and similar. Interpreting in courts and tribunals can be reasonably regarded as being consecutive interpreting in the conference setting. In general, there is a pronounced element of 'performance'; the interpreter is performing as a speaker in public and is the focus of the audience's attention.

Usually the languages used are decided upon ahead of time so that interpreters can be organized. It is not unusual to have up to four languages in these circumstances. The interpreters are seated where they are able to have eye contact with all participants. As each intervention by a participant is completed, the interpreters will, in turn, interpret into the other languages of the group. If, for example, the languages are French, German and Italian, and a French speaker's statement or point of view will be interpreted into German and Italian, three interpreters would be used, one having French, one German and one Italian as their 'mother' tongue or working language.

The length of the speeches varies, but often the interpreter is expected to handle up to six or seven minutes of speech. Interpreters often need to remind speakers to keep their interventions to a reasonable length, especially since it is not usual practice to interrupt or to ask the speaker to present the material in segments. This helps the flow of communication, as the audience has to wait for interpretation into the other languages before the debate can advance.

The size of the audience varies; in the above example, thirty or forty would not be uncommon, possibly down to ten or twelve. In the case of more formal functions and after-dinner speeches, the audience may be augmented by press, television and other guests.

Equipment such as microphones, recorders and slides are often used, and the interpreter has to make adjustments to techniques in order to cater for them; for instance, it is advisable to obtain copies of overhead transparencies from the speaker beforehand since it is often difficult to see them clearly enough for the purposes of interpreting.

Consecutive interpreting in liaison settings is characterized by the interpreter having at least two clients, each speaking a different language. In some cases there are more than two clients but they still constitute two language groups.

The *physical environment* as well as a different degree of formality makes for a more intimate setting than usually applies with conferences. One consequence of this physical environment is greater difficulty in clearly delineating role and recognizing the boundary between the interpreting function and other activities. (see Chapter 3) The positioning of the interpreter between the clients is directed to clarifying for all parties who is responsible for communication. In such situations as doctor/patient consultations this may seem superfluous, but experience shows that even where particular and well accepted expertise being sought by the client, the tendency for clients to abdicate responsibility to the interpreter is strong—despite the often-enunciated fear on the part of clients of losing control over the interview.

Normally, the liaison interpreter interprets after the client has finished speaking, then listens to the intervention by the second client and interprets this to the first. The length of the segments can be substantial but is generally shorter than in consecutive interpreting in conference settings. The *immediacy* places an added responsibility on the interpreter: when one client finishes speaking, this is not to be taken as an indication that they have no more to say in that exchange. Often one interlocutor pauses in order to allow for the interpretation, and the other interlocutor takes it as a signal to respond. The interpreter, who is the only one aware of the intention of the speakers, thus has to intervene to a certain extent in the dynamic of the communication in order to help it flow in the most economical and efficient fashion.

A further complication arises from *interruptions* during the interpretation; one of the clients is reacting to a portion of what the other has said before hearing the full rendition. A reaction to part of a reply is likely to produce confusion and lead to questions being asked of the interpreter, who is then forced to provide explanations and clarifications which are time-consuming and lead to questioning of the interpreter's competence.

The *length of segments* requires particular attention even if only to dispel certain misconceptions. There is no absolute measure of the length of segments; the overall criterion is the necessity to allow the speakers to express themselves freely, at their own rhythm and pace. In all but the most unusual circumstances this means allowing them to finish the question or comment without interruption and then interpreting the whole segment at a speed which is slightly faster than the original. This provides for an efficient exchange of ideas and sets the interpreter's input apart, in that the source language segments will be characterized by the natural pauses and hesitations which are part of speech when the speaker is formulating and developing ideas without any preparation. In other words, the clients are producing utterances which are formulated to be heard, not written to be read. The interpreter has heard the complete utterance before being required to interpret it whereas the clients are constructing the text as they go along.

When the interpreter needs to interrupt before either client has completed a segment, the following elements need to be considered: the interpreter should interrupt at the end of a 'sense group', i.e. at a point where a natural break would occur because of the completion of a particular idea or point being made; after the interpretation, the interpreter should indicate by eye contact or posture a return to the original client to allow the client to continue; the interpreter should not interrupt at the crucial points of the speaker's remarks.

That the *size of the audience* is much smaller than in conference settings provides opportunities but also creates some problems. On the one hand, the more intimate situation can allow the interpreter occasionally to seek the repetition of a segment which has been misheard or not fully comprehended, without major embarrassment. On the other hand, the interpreter can easily become involved to an extent which can impair professional performance; the absence of colleagues can deprive the interpreter of feedback and place the interpreter in a position of considerable power *vis-à-vis* the clients. The judicious exercise of this power is part of the interpreter's professional obligations.

Certain situations demand particular techniques and specific behaviour. Later chapters will look at these aspects; this general section deals with situations where an interpreter works with more than two clients. In an educational counselling session, for example—where on one side one might have the parents of a child who is the object of the session, and on the other an educational counsellor, a careers teacher and an educational psychologist—the interpreter must lay down some *ground rules* if the counselling session is going to achieve any worthwhile purpose. Since it may not be clear who takes turns to speak, and two speakers of the same language may make successive interventions without the interpreter having an opportunity to interpret, the interpretation must be prefaced by some attribution of the source of the remarks about to be interpreted. This will tend to augment the artificiality of the situation but is a necessary technique if the clients are to be aware of who has said what. As a rule, consecutive interpreting is done in the first person, i.e. the interpreter speaks as the person who has made the remarks, but in such situations as that described above, this rule may be broken to avoid chaos, especially when emotions run high and interjections are frequent.

The interpreter must control the interpreting situation, not as an exercise of power over the direction or the conduct of the interaction but as a measure of management of the situation *because* it involves an interpreter. The clients must not talk over each other, must be clear about the fact that they are talking to each other and *not* to the interpreter, and the interpreter must not be used as a source of further opinion or as an arbiter.

Simultaneous interpreting in liaison settings is used in particular circumstances and is mostly 'chuchotage'—a variant of simultaneous interpreting performed without the use of interpreting booths or other technical equipment and with the interpreter sitting behind and whispering to the client (or clients, usually no more than two or three) while the speaker continues with the delivery of the communication without reference to the interpreter. While this technique has particular applications and obvious limitations, it is used quite consistently in liaison settings where members of the audience need to be informed of what is being said but their own intervention is either inappropriate or impossible. In discussion of the mental health and legal fields this variant will be further illustrated; at this point it is useful to note that it is particularly suited to liaison settings where spoken discourse is the element through which a diagnosis is made or the means by which power is exercised over the listeners.

Note-taking

Not long after the beginnings of the interpreting profession, a number of practitioners turned their attention to devising a method of note-taking suitable for consecutive interpreting. The seminal work in this area is Rozan (1956). Our comments apply to liaison interpreting situations.

Note-taking is a legitimate activity in any type of consecutive interpreting and does not reflect negatively on the interpreter's ability. On the contrary, it is an indication of the interpreter's interest in providing the best service for the clients. While in some circumstances note-taking will be essential, in others it is completely out of place and indeed detrimental. In mental health situations, for instance, note-taking is best avoided as the presence of a third person taking notes is likely to arouse the suspicion of the patient and lead to a breakdown in the assessment or therapeutic process. In a court of law, the public performance of the interpreter usually precludes resorting to notes as the interpreter is usually standing and has nowhere to place note-pads.

Generally speaking, note-taking should be encouraged, and indeed contributes to a much clearer definition of the interpreter's role. The mere act of taking notes reinforces the role of the interpreter as relaying someone else's message. Furthermore, this idiosyncratic visual representation of the message on paper serves the purpose of ensuring that the interpreting is complete, that names and figures are rendered accurately, that the coherence and cohesion of the argument are reproduced and that the chances of omissions are reduced.

Arguments in the literature over the use of symbols and the creation of a personalized set of symbols are in a sense superfluous, since the acid test for any set of notes is the quality of the interpreting which ensues; it matters little what the notes look like. However, some principles are important. The rules for abbreviation, the layout of the notes and other principles need to be practised consistently to improve the quality of the interpreting.

The level of note-taking must be tailored to the particular situation. Excessive preoccupation with note-taking creates difficulties with the dynamics of liaison interpreting situations where the interpreter is seen as someone who writes furiously and subsequently reads from the notes. The technique must be unobtrusive and the emphasis must remain on the face-to-face communication which is the hallmark of liaison interpreting. Furthermore, excessive note-taking may lead the interpreter to miss the point of the exchange. It is incumbent upon the interpreter to abandon the notes and rely on grasping the idea being communicated: this is the absolute priority.

Shorthand is often suggested as a method of ensuring completeness of the notes. However, this practice is inimical to the task of interpreting as it substitutes for the language of the speaker another system of signs which represent a third 'language'. A 'translation' of the notes is thus necessary, and the stilted performance which this produces mitigates against the information processing role which is central to interpreting.

Memory

The role of memory in interpreting in general, and in liaison interpreting in particular, is complex and little understood. Novice interpreters often believe a 'good memory' to be the *sine qua non* of good interpreting, but it is worth noting that in liaison interpreting memory is used to recall information received only one or two minutes before. One is not dealing with the recall of facts, events and situations which occurred years before; nor is one dealing with 'trace' memory whereby items of information are recalled for a very short time and then forgotten—as when a phone number is relayed from one person to another, and promptly forgotten after it has been dialled.

The role of memory in interpreting relates to the ability to make connections between what is said and what one already knows about the subject matter. In short, it is easier to understand and retain what can be easily incorporated into our previous knowledge of certain topics. Since the first and most important phase of interpreting is understanding what the client is saying, memory has more to do with the preparation for an interpreting task than with the raw ability to commit to memory the utterance being spoken. It is our view that rather than seeking improvements to memory, we can best improve the performance of the interpreting task by developing a repertoire of knowledge which is the product of intense curiosity about our environment, whether we are intrinsically interested in the topic or not.

Sources of stress

Expectations of the role of the interpreter within environments which are at times inimical to the very existence of interpreting are the first and perhaps main source of stress. The clients' expectations may conflict with the interpreter's view of the professional role. Reliance on the interpreter to be advocate, cultural expert, guide and buffer between the hegemonic culture and that of the other client is the most likely source of stress.

Lack of recognition or lack of adequate reward for the task performed is a second, and related, source of stress. Apart from the strictly monetary aspect of this, frustration derives from the treatment of the interpreter as a 'tap' to be turned on or off at will, with an almost total disregard for the needs of the interpreter in terms of preparation for an assignment and subsequent debriefing.

Lack of opportunity to measure oneself against one's peers, is a third source of stress. Since the work is performed mostly by individuals and seldom by teams, the interpreter is left wondering about the standards being applied and consequently unsure about their own performance *vis-à-vis* that of other interpreters.

Lastly, environmental factors may induce stress—environment including physical as well as emotional elements. Interpreting in a noisy factory or a police lock-up or at the bedside of a dying patient are all examples of stressful environments.

3 The Role of the Interpreter

Because the interpreter is a participant, and thus has a presence, in the liaison interpreting situation, the question of role must be considered in detail. This chapter deals with the essential elements of role, the perception of this role and the effects of these perceptions not only on the interpreter but also on the clients. The relationship between social context and role are examined as are, in conclusion, some differences between translation and interpreting in relation to role.

Defining the role

Role is a social science construct used to explain behaviour and examine attitudes between at least two participants in any social situation. The concept of role is inextricably tied to the idea of a reciprocal relationship; thus dyads exist such as doctor/patient, teacher/pupil, lawyer/client, etc. The essential point is that each of these roles exists only in relation to the other. Thus a teacher can only be a teacher when there is a pupil to be taught; the role of a doctor only becomes evident in the presence of a patient. The common perception of role as a part which a person plays in a given situation is often used in the realm of entertainment, such as theatre. This construct is useful in liaison interpreting situations to describe

3 THE ROLE OF THE INTERPRETER

not only the relationship and attitudes of the clients to each other but also the relationships between the interpreter and each client in turn.

The role of the interpreter, like other roles, derives from observed behaviour over time and from evaluation of behaviour *vis-à-vis* that expected by professional associations or other occupational or social groupings. Since the operations of liaison interpreters have been little studied, and not much interest has been shown in the social dimension of liaison interpreting, the construction of the role has occurred in a fairly haphazard and unco-ordinated manner. This has created significant professional and ethical problems for the interpreter.

The mere presence of the interpreter provokes human reaction to the presence of another person. There are tendencies to treat the interpreter as a third interlocutor; for clients to treat each other as somewhat removed from the situation both when speaking to each other and when awaiting the interpretation; and to treat the interpreter as an evaluator of information and thus a client advocate. Such expectations by each client of the interpreter's role may be incompatible with the professional obligations of the interpreter. In short, there are complex interactions between the interpreter and each client, between the clients themselves, and between the interpreter and each client as representatives of particular social groupings.

There are *two dimensions* to the interpreter's role. The interpreter's own attitudes towards that role can be defined as the 'ideographic dimension'; the expectations and attitudes which a social system, variously defined, has of the interpreter can be referred to as the 'nomothetic dimension' (after Getzels, 1958). In a hospital setting, for example, the ideographic dimension would include all the interpreter's misgivings about the nature of the situation, the context of health and sickness, and the physical conditions of the work; the nomothetic dimension encompasses the attitude of the hospital as employer (whether the interpreter is employed on a casual or full-time basis) and its expectations of the interpreter. The interpreter may be seen by the hospital as a 'helper' in the care of patients and so be assigned tasks which are appropriate to the general category of 'helper' but are not interpreting tasks. If the interpreter consistently accedes to these requests, the role thus constructed contains elements which fall clearly outside accepted professional performance. A kaleidoscope of roles thus developed is not conducive to the creation of professional identity, ethical standards and *esprit de corps* amongst interpreters.

It is clear then, that the role of the interpreter evolves within two distinct but inextricably intertwined dimensions: the interpreting function itself, and the context in which that function is performed. The practitioner must make a clear differentiation between the context and the task; it is not a matter of keeping these two dimensions separate, but of evaluating to what extent the functional task is modified or extended by the particular context. Decisions must be made on the likely corruption of the communication function if the contextual influences are allowed to dictate behaviour beyond a certain point.

Comparisons with other professional and social roles

As in other professional roles, a *reciprocal relationship* is taken for granted. But the interpreter must maintain this role in relation to *two* clients and continually switch between them. Consequently, each client must not see the interpreter as a conveyor of information between client and interpreter, but must accept the interaction for what it is: a discussion between clients. Thus the interpreter's role is both vicarious (being performed on somebody else's behalf) and in effect a double role (being performed for two clients).

Contextual factors contribute to a role which differs from other professional and social roles. Interpreters must, at all costs, regard themselves as the instrument rather than the focus of the communication. In real situations this task is extremely difficult. The physical proximity of the interpreter to the clients is one factor which contributes to the difficulty of keeping this 'distance'.

The first problem is that the relationship between client and interpreter extends beyond the interpreting situation. Thus preliminaries such as greetings, directions, briefings are carried out on a one-to-one basis with each client, either in person or by telephone. Other spatial and temporal circumstances can add to the difficulties. If, for example, a doctor is late for an appointment and the interpreter is left with the patient in an ante-room, the natural tendency is for the patient to engage in social conversation with the interpreter, possibly about matters which will form part of the consultation with the doctor. This inevitably changes the client's expectations of the doctor/patient interaction. The patient may respond differently to questions by the doctor in the expectation that the interpreter will supplement them with information already provided by the patient. If the doctor is in an analogous situation, then the doctor's expectations may change similarly.

Here the role of the interpreter is created not during or because of but outside the performance of the interpreting function. While the intentions of the clients are honourable, they place the interpreter in the invidious situation of having to deal with a discrepancy in the expectations of the interpreter and each of the clients.

Other issues related to the presence of the interpreter are even more likely to affect the long-term view of the interpreter by the clients. At many points during the interpreting situation, the interpreter has the role of 'participant-observer', particularly if either or both clients are unhappy with the progress of the discussion. The first tendency is to question the role of the interpreter in the interaction, either by direct questioning of the interpreter or by suggestions as to how to move the interaction along—or occasionally by direct requests of opinion from the interpreter. When the clients cease talking to or focusing on each other, they inevitably impinge on the function of the interpreter by identifying with the interpreter as a person. The situation is further complicated when underlying factors favour identification by one client or the other, such as organisational affiliation (doctor and interpreter may work in the same hospital), ethnic identity (patient and interpreter may belong to the same ethnic group) or who is paying the interpreter.

Status differential between clients and between the client and the interpreter will impinge on the interpreter's role. In conference interpreting this issue seldom arises, due both to the physical separation of interpreter and interlocutors, and to the fact that most situations involve groups of people with similar educational and social experiences who wish to communicate. Where the status and educational background of the clients is vastly different, a great deal more energy has to be expended in order to make the communication work. If shared assumptions about the world do not obtain, the interpreter is often implicitly required to bridge such gaps.

It becomes a question of great delicacy as to how far the interpreter should go. For example, in some societies doctors hold either higher or lower status than in the country where the interpreting is taking place; thus certain patient attitudes or behaviours may not be understood by the doctor. The interpreter has to make immediate choices in terms of conveying these attitudes in the speech or the gestures of the doctor or the patient. But is it the role of the interpreter to intervene in a didactic fashion if and when problems of this kind surface? The negative consequences of such intervention to the performance of the interpreting task must be clearly understood by the interpreter before embarking on such action.

The perception of the role of the interpreter is also affected by *language issues*. The approach to the task of interpreting and its perception is often coloured by the facility and speed with which interpreting takes place. For each of the clients, the way in which the interpreter delivers the message is as important as the message itself. If the interpreter's performance indicates that the interpreting is a necessary and decisive component of the communication situation, then his or her role in bridging the communication gap is conveyed unambiguously. Hesitations, requests for repetitions and indications of being unsure and ill at ease will colour the clients' perceptions of the role of the interpreter in terms of their expectation of the accuracy and the mode of delivery of the message. Rate of delivery, manner of delivery and capacity to inspire confidence are usually described in terms of language competence. While this alignment is questionable, nevertheless these factors are of paramount importance in the perceptions of the role of the interpreter.

The interpreting interaction

In this section an interpreted interaction will be examined with a view to highlighting the aspects which impinge on the role of the interpreter.

3 THE ROLE OF THE INTERPRETER

We can assume that there is *motivation* to communicate for the achievement of goals which are shared, at least to some extent, by the interlocutors. This implies a number of features such as the linear ones common to all communication between two people—namely the tendency to 'turn-taking', the necessity for a feedback loop, the inevitable 'noise' and other common possibilities and pitfalls. The features peculiar to an interpreted interaction can be looked at as a 'normal' communication situation with two loops, one which involves client 1 and the interpreter and the other which involves client 2 and the interpreter.

However, this model does not actually reflect the dynamics of an interpreted situation. The motivation and the need for communication stem from both clients and not the interpreter; and the elements of communication flow will not necessarily operate in the same manner when the interaction is interpreted. The interposition of an interpreter creates what could be termed an 'unnatural' situation which both clients recognize and would prefer did not exist.

The *time element*, or its perception, is an important feature. Assuming perfect performance by the interpreter, an interpreted interaction must take much longer than a conversation between two people who share a language. On the other hand, both interlocutors accept that communication other than with these arrangements would not be possible at all, and make adjustments. Some of these are positive, as far as the interpreter is concerned, while others are negative.

Take, for example, the concept of *turn-taking*. Ordinarily the speakers follow a fairly constant pattern of turn-taking; interruption of one party by the other is a risk to communication since it does not allow the other party to finish their contribution. Any misunderstandings arising out of a departure from alternating turns are generally solved during the next turn or by the insistence of one party in continuing their turn. In an interpreted situation, such departures from rigid turn-taking become a problem. It is impossible for the interpreter to operate when two people are talking over each other; the interpreter must exercise some control over the situation and the most common method is to ensure that the interlocutors speak in turn. This method forces the presentation of material in a manner which will elicit the most productive response from the other party. It also assumes that the end of each intervention represents the end of that client's input on that topic, whereas the break may reflect the perceived ability of the interpreter to cope. The result is often detrimental to the spontaneity of the interaction and leaves the interlocutors unhappy about the role of the interpreter. This effect is produced regardless of the quality of the interpreter's performance.

A further aspect of the time element is the interval during which each client is not directly and cognitively engaged—when the interpreter is relaying an utterance to the other person and that person is replying. These '*pauses*', while inevitable, work against a constant and focused flow of communication. They may cause a client to believe that the response is not connected to the question as asked; the client is unsure as to whether this discrepancy arises from the interpreter's work or the other party. Again these perceptions impinge upon the creation and evaluation of the role of the interpreter.

Asides and comments or questions may be directed at the interpreter who has considerable difficulty in interpreting all that is referred to him or her while recognizing that the asides are just that.

In summary, the structural requirements of the interpreted interaction are sometimes counterproductive in terms of communication outcomes, thus negatively affecting the perception of the role of the interpreter. Furthermore, the clients' lack of familiarity with these consequences promotes negative impressions of the interpreter. Once those who work with interpreters are familiar with the issues, the problems can be drastically reduced.

The concept of 'client'

An interpreter has at least two clients at any one time. Theoretically they have equal claim on the interpreter's expertise, irrespective of considerations such as who arranged for the interpreter to be present, who is paying the interpreter, who has briefed the interpreter. The reality is often different. It is likely that the person who arranged for the interpreter to be present will consider themselves to be the client, and perceptions about the role of the interpreter will be governed by this presumed relationship. It is true that in certain contexts—usually business contexts—the idea of an interpreter 'working for' one of the clients is not only taken for granted but seen as a condition of employment of the interpreter. Such situations embody potential conflict between the interpreter as a 'servant' of one master, and the ethical imperatives of interpreting where impartiality and confidentiality are axiomatic.

The concept of client relies on an understanding of the fundamental part which an interpreter plays in an interaction. It is precisely because there is no such general understanding amongst potential clients that this is an issue at all. It is understandable that the person calling an interpreter feels that, by expressing a need to communicate with the other person, they have taken the initiative and have the right to some measure of control over the interpreter. In most cases, the employment of an interpreter is, from the clients' point of view, a rare event. There is little motivation for these clients to be sympathetic to the interpreter's concerns—especially since there can be no measure of how such a concern might have affected outcomes.

Creation of the role

The creation of a role for interpreters must also be approached from a global perspective which seeks to place, in operational terms, the professional obligations which interpreters have to their clients and to their professional colleagues. Liaison interpreting cannot yet rely on long-standing common practices and agreed guidelines within a closely controlled industrial framework. Something approaching this framework does exists for conference interpreters. However, the work of liaison interpreters covers such a variety of situations, and is often performed in such an *ad hoc* manner by untrained and sometimes unwilling practitioners, that it is difficult to specify behaviour requirements. Further, the enforcement of such guidelines, where they exist, relies almost solely on the professionalism of the practitioners—who usually work in isolation and so must rely on themselves for evaluation. We regard it as axiomatic that clarification of the role of the interpreter will lead to increased professionalism and a better service to clients.

The first element which affects the view of the interpreter's role is *the question of language*. A liaison interpreter, unlike a conference interpreter, operates not from a number of languages into their 'mother' tongue (or the language in which they received the bulk of their education) but both into and out of their 'mother' tongue (A language) and their second (B) language (the classification also extends to C languages). Competence in the second language needs to be of a very high order. Clients, who are generally not familiar with the intricacies of the classification of languages for interpreting, expect the same level of performance in both directions. They probably also lack an appreciation of the nature of language and the difficulties inherent in the transfer of a message from one language to another. This fact assumes significant proportions where the context of the interpreting does not begin to take such issues into account—for example, a court of law, a psychiatric assessment interview or business negotiations.

The clients see the interpreter as a 'language converter', not as someone who is concerned with communication; hence the model of a tap which can be turned on and off at will and which will produce language, any language. The interpreter is seen only in terms of language competence and, conversely, the assumption is made that language competence is tantamount to interpreting competence. Furthermore, the client's regard is likely to depend on the number of languages they believe the interpreter speaks!

If this language competence issue is to be placed in its proper perspective, we must specify other skills which differentiate the work of an interpreter from that of a bilingual. Whether performed in the simultaneous or the consecutive mode, liaison interpreting involves operations on the *message* and not on the language. The essence of interpreting skills is to receive a message which is not formulated for the interpreter and to deliver that message in a form and a character indistinguishable from the original. The message includes all the elements which constitute the act of communication (comprising semantic, pragmatic and semiotic dimensions) in a particular temporal and situational context. The skills of an interpreter therefore extend beyond the linguistic and include the capacity to internalize and transmit the many nuances of a particular situation. Note-taking skills are also essential, and a series of other skills relating to the *management* but not the *conduct* of an interpreted interaction.

The interpreter also needs the ability to *empathize* with each interlocutor in turn at each exchange, and to enter the particular situation in such a way as to appear 'natural' to the interlocutors. This requires a well-developed technique of familiarization with the context of the assignment by research and backgrounding strategies geared to produce quick, precise results and to be flexible in less predictable circumstances. Thus, the interpreter needs not only a reservoir of excellent general knowledge, but an awareness of how this knowledge is handled in both the source and target languages, both conceptually and linguistically.

Translating and interpreting

Within the literature, much is assumed and little said about the differences between the two skills, apart from the fact that translation involves written texts and interpreting involves oral ones. When one is dealing with clients, however, this distinction is blurred by a number of factors which, in turn, contribute to clients' perceptions of the roles of interpreters and translators.

Halliday (1981) is a useful starting point for discussing consequences of the differences between the two functions. i.e. interpreting and translating. Two issues emerge as significant. The first is lack of consistency within the profession in the use of the two terms: sometimes the distinction between written and oral text is respected; sometimes the terms 'translation' and 'translator' incorporate the notion of 'interpreting' and 'interpreter'. The second concerns the interpreter often being asked to perform 'sight translation', whereby a written document relevant to the situation (for example, a lawyer/client interview) is passed to the interpreter for immediate oral 'translation'. One can argue that this activity straddles the two professional roles, as do others such as subtitling or surtitling. Indeed there are some areas of professional activity which cannot be classified easily as interpreting or translating. The crucial point, which is most relevant to role construction, is that the clients are not aware of these distinctions and may have unreasonable expectations of the interpreter hired to perform either function.

The differences between the two skills are often characterized in terms of the level of accuracy which can be expected from each. The typical view is that the immediacy of interpreting merits a less stringent approach to accuracy—defined both as completeness of message transfer and attention to nuance. Such views reflect a failure, whether deliberate or otherwise, to recognize that indeed the two activities require different skills and different aptitudes. The differences are not so much in the performance of the activities as in the nature of oral and written texts. In creating the role of interpreter or translator we must contend with these misapprehensions as well as with the well-worn and popular conception that language competence is the same as interpreting or translating competence.

In summary, the role of the liaison interpreter is governed by a matrix of dimensions, some to do with the interpreters themselves and some with the clients' level of knowledge of the function. The central issue is the complex interaction between the activity which the interpreter performs, the way this is seen by the clients and the way the profession itself sees the role as developing.

The interpreter's aim is that the interaction resemble as closely as possible the same interaction where an interpreter is not required. But this linear approach is hardly ever possible. While the interpreter persists with this objective, the clients see the physical presence of the interpreter as leading to serious and often deleterious consequences for the communication. Overlying this situation is the fact that interpreters have little opportunity to discuss experiences and must evaluate their own performance and attempt to generalize from them. It is easier to consider each interaction as 'peculiar' and to defer the important task of drawing together the broader lessons.

4 The Interpreted Interview

The term 'interview' refers to a whole range of face-to-face situations where interpreting takes place; for example, any professional/client interview, doctor/patient consultations, parent/teacher meetings, public service user/provider interviews, business individual or team negotiations etc.

Objectives of the interview

Essentially, the presence of an interpreter does not change the objective of the interview: to accomplish some necessary/real life task. For example, a doctor/patient interview usually aims at diagnosis, treatment, prognosis, follow-up etc.; a parent/teacher interview aims at discussing some issue related to a child's schooling, providing insights as to why there is a problem, trying to solve the problem; a family therapy session aims at identifying and solving social, emotional, psychological etc. problems; a trade (business) negotiation interview aims at agreement on investment, buying and selling, setting up joint ventures etc. In other words, an interpreter usually walks into a situation where the other parties have already determined why the interview is necessary, what the parameters will be, the specific objective and the steps to be taken to achieve it (Tebble, 1991, 1993). An interpreted interview does not have different objectives; the essential character of the interview does not change because an interpreter is necessary.

The only differences are practical ones, such as the length of time it takes for the interview to be completed and the dynamics of the fact that the parties involved cannot respond spontaneously to each other.

Ideally, the parties in the interview—other than the interpreter—should speak in as natural a way as possible, as if they are communicating with each other in the same language. In reality, people sometimes find that the very presence of an interpreter creates stress, which affects the way they speak or address each other. For example, they may speak to and keep eye contact with the interpreter, who speaks their language, rather than with their interlocutor. Or they may preface what they say by 'Tell him/her that . . .' instead of saying it directly. The trained interpreter is, of course, able to deal with such problems, but it is best to educate people in how to work with interpreters on such issues.

The interpreter's objective is to effect as accurately as possible the communication between the parties. The first and most important role is as a bilingual professional, whose ability to transfer meanings from one language to the other makes the communication possible. However, other factors may impinge. There may be cultural, professional, institutional, organizational etc. aspects involved in an interview which require some input from the interpreter, who has the requisite knowledge alongside linguistic and message transfer skills.

It takes a high level of language skills as well as interpreting skills to achieve such communication, and the objectives of an interview will not be met adequately if the interpreter lacks either. The two are not the same. *Language skills* have to do with the ability to use language correctly in any given context: grammatically, lexically, syntactically, fluently, idiomatically etc. *Interpreting skills* have to do with the ability to correctly transfer meanings from one language into another. The onus is on the interpreter to maintain a high level of language and interpreting skills. It is unethical to accept work when one's skills are not up to scratch.

The yardstick against which one measures the success of the interpreted interview is the interview not requiring an interpreter. For example, the outcome of a parent/teacher interview where the teacher and the parent speak different languages should be the same as of a parent/teacher interview where they speak the same language. All parties should go away feeling happy that they were able to discuss, ask questions and get answers to those questions, and that there are no residual matters due to the fact that an interpreter had to be present. If an interpreted interview does not achieve this, then the objectives of the interview have not been met.

The interpreter and the other parties

The interpreter may work in an extremely wide range of situations, and with and for a variety of people. In certain institutional settings, such as hospitals and government departments, the interpreter may be a permanent member of staff or at least a regular member of a team involving other professionals—doctors, nurses, teachers, social workers, policemen etc. In these situations, interpreting may be needed regularly or occasionally. Preparation for such interviews involves minimum effort on the part of the interpreter who is familiar with the domain and knows and has worked with most of the other professionals and their clients before. Briefing is often unnecessary; even if a case is a one-off, the amount of preparation will be fairly brief, although the interpreter will need to look into the specific details of each case.

In situations such as legal interpreting and police work, the interpreter may be a regular who is familiar with the professionals and the domain, but the other parties will usually be unknown and briefing will be necessary. Of course, a legal or police case may evolve into a long-term one where the interpreter becomes so familiar with it that briefing and preparation again become almost unnecessary. In both these cases the objectives of the interview may not be difficult to fulfil.

Freelance interpreters or those working through agencies may be given a wide range of assignments, often on a daily basis. Either the professional or the other party may employ the interpreter, i.e. pay for services. In some cases the other party may be familiar with the domain and the professionals, in others they may be quite unfamiliar with both. It is imperative that the interpreter find out as much as possible about each case and do any reading, researching, vocabulary preparation etc. necessary to enable him/her to fulfil the objectives of the interview, which is to facilitate effective communication.

Whatever the situation, the interpreter must attempt three things: *briefing, introductions and debriefing*. We say 'attempt' because in reality things are not always ideal: professionals may be in a hurry or not particularly motivated by ethical considerations; professionals and clients may not know how to work with interpreters; clients may be stressed and apprehensive. However, briefing and debriefing are necessary parts of any professional/client interview and should not be skipped over (Tebble, 1991: 57–8). Things may go quite wrong in an interview as a result of no briefing. For example, relevant or key information may not come to light, and people may make all sorts of inappropriate assumptions. Briefing helps to explain the dimensions of the interview to all parties and establishes the grounds upon which it is based, all of which is good preparation for the communicative process. Debriefing helps to resolve any residual problems and to decide whether another interview is necessary.

Even if briefing is not possible the interpreter must at least attempt to introduce everybody. Professional courtesy helps to create a feeling of trust and professionalism which affects positively the attitudes of the participants towards each other. Positive attitudes generally make for positive communicative situations.

Getting the message

Effective interpreting requires effective *listening skills*. A distinction must be made between hearing and listening. *Hearing*—or the automatic ability to receive sounds—is a sensory aspect which alone is not enough to enable an interpreter to 'get the message', i.e. to understand the meaning of an utterance. *Listening*, on the other hand, is a totally conscious process demanding attention and concentration.

4 THE INTERPRETED INTERVIEW

Listening for meaning consists of locating the logical connections or relationships in an utterance, not simply understanding the meanings of words. The interpreter will not understand the meanings of utterances unless he/she listens for these logical connections (Larson, 1984: 3).

Understanding the speaker is not only the first step in the process of interpreting, but also the most crucial one. The interpreter must understand before he/she can produce anything sensible (Feldweg, 1989). So, interpreters must not be perceived as walking 'bilingual dictionaries'. All the vocabulary and terminology in the world will be useless unless the interpreter has the linguistic structures (syntax, grammar, logical connections) to hang the words on.

Understanding by listening for logical connections is also crucial to the way memory operates. It is far easier to remember a spoken text whose logical structure you have understood than one whose structure you have not grasped. Experiments have shown that people are better at recalling semantic content, i.e. the basic logical connections in a text, than the lexical items used in the text.

Once the interpreter has developed effective listening skills, he/she is able to deal with other aspects which affect understanding, such as vagueness, lack of clarity, difficulty. It is perfectly appropriate for the interpreter to seek clarification, explanations etc. from the speakers during the interview, but only when the speakers have created problems of comprehension, not simply as a way of covering up the interpreter's lack of concentration or other problems. If the interpreter needs clarification or explanation, he/she must let the party from whom the clarification/explanation is *not* sought know what is going on. Failure to do this may lead to assumptions that there is collusion between the interpreter and the party from whom the clarification *is* sought, leading perhaps to lack of trust in the interpreter and the latter party.

It is far worse to misinterpret or distort a meaning because a necessary clarification or explanation was not sought than to interrupt the flow of the interview in order to seek such clarification/explanation. People who are familiar with working with interpreters usually take questions of this kind from interpreters as a sign of professionalism, of caring about 'getting it right', provided they arise only from a genuine difficulty not of the interpreter's making and not from a lack of language and/or interpreting skills on the part of the interpreter.

Interrupting a speaker who goes on for too long is also an appropriate course of action. But, again, it must be done carefully and only when there is too much material to be handled in one go, not as a means of covering up for a lack of skills. Liaison interpreters are expected to cope with spoken texts of several sentences at a time, not just one. They are expected to cope with complex logical sequences and syntactically sophisticated utterances. The interpreter does not abruptly stop a speaker mid-sentence because he/she thinks that's enough. On the other hand, if out of excessive politeness or timidity the interpreter allows any speaker to go on and on, there are two possible outcomes, both negative in terms of the objectives of the interview. Either the segment will be abbreviated or summarised, or the interpreter will ask the speaker to repeat the whole thing. The former will damage the integrity of the meaning and the latter will slow down the flow of the interview. Both are greater prices to pay than a polite request by the interpreter to the speaker to stop at a logical point. Clarifications, explanations and interruptions, then, are often necessary steps in fulfilling the objective of the interview: effective communication.

The issue of dialects will be addressed briefly. In certain contexts, the criterion of 'mutual intelligibility' (Trudgill, 1981: 13ff.) does not apply. In the case of Italian and its dialects, for example, non-speakers of a particular dialect do not normally understand that dialect and cannot be expected to interpret it. If the interpreter does not know beforehand that a dialect will be used, he/she may deal with the situation in a number of ways. The interpreter may repeat in the standard language the dialect speaker's message for that speaker to verify content etc., but this will slow down the interview considerably. The interpreter who can understand but not speak the dialect can use the standard language while the speaker of the dialect uses the dialect. If at all possible, however, the interpreter should not accept that assignment, especially if he/she knew beforehand that a dialect would be used. The interpreter may suggest a colleague who is a speaker of that dialect or, if nobody can be found, at least make it clear to the other parties in the interview that there is a problem.

Transmitting the message

Just as effective *listening* skills are necessary for the interpreter to be able to 'get the message', effective *speaking* skills are necessary to transmit the message. Effective speaking skills range from quality of voice to choice of idiom, vocabulary, phrasing etc. So both what comes out of the mouth of the interpreter and the way it comes out are important in the overall effectiveness of the interpretation.

The interpreter must develop clear *speaking skills*. Some interpreters are naturally gifted in this area; others may have to work at it through training and practice. The interpreter should speak loudly enough to be audible to all parties—neither yelling nor whispering. Although the speed of the interpreter's two languages may not be the same, the delivery must be neither too fast nor too slow. Speed must not be confused with *fluency*, for which the interpreter must aim. Fluency consists of correct pace, intonation, stress, tone and an absence of false starts, repetitions, pauses and hesitation. So an interpreter may 'sound slow' but may nevertheless be perfectly fluent. The speed of the interpretation often depends, of course, on the delivery of the speakers. Pauses, hesitation, inflections, nuance must all be interpreted, as they constitute an inherent part of the total meaning.

The level of language usage is often referred to as *register* (Fromkin, 1990: 265). Human beings, through socialization, choose language according to the communicative situation they are in. In other words, the way we speak to our family and friends at home is different to the way we speak to our colleagues at work or to a professional we are consulting in a professional capacity. We may be talking about the same thing but the way we talk about it will differ. Levels of language usage have been described in various ways by linguists and sociolinguists, but generally we can talk about casual, informal, formal, standard, specialized etc. levels of usage.

Register is a matter of both syntax and lexis. For example, in English the use of the passive voice is generally considered to be more formal than the use of the active voice (although there are rules of grammar governing the usage of both). Lexical register is very much determined by the specific communicative context. I can talk about 'dad', 'daddy', 'papa' etc. when I'm talking to a close friend or relative. But in a professional situation, such as a job interview or a medical consultation, I can only use the word 'father'. It is often believed that professionals use the register of their professions when dealing with their clients. In fact, professionals talk to their clients in a variety of ways ranging from professional (specialist even) register to quite colloquial register—from the solicitor's 'A caveat has been placed by the vendor's creditors on the said property' to the urologist's 'How's the waterworks today?'

The question is not how the professionals and their clients choose to speak, i.e. what register they employ, but how the interpreter deals with it. It is often assumed that a professional can speak as he/she wishes and that the interpreter should modify that message to suit the client, since the interpreter presumably 'knows' that client's language and culture. It is dangerous to make assumptions about the speakers of any language and their culture, as stereotypes are often inaccurate and misleading. An interpreter must not talk 'up' or 'down' at anyone receiving the interpreting service. And modifying what any professional has said can be a dangerous practice, as rephrasing can change and distort the message unacceptably. So the registers used by the professionals and their speakers must be maintained by the interpreter. The formulation of the message is the responsibility of the other parties; the interpreter's responsibility is to interpret.

Ideally these things should be cleared up during briefing, especially in situations of freelance or one-off interpreting where the interpreter has not worked with the other parties before and may not know whether they are familiar with interpreters. Requests from professionals to 'tell him or her such and such' must be politely but firmly refused. If a situation like this arises, the interpreter must take steps immediately to explain that the interpreter is there to interpret and not to 'tell people'. If, on the other hand, the interpreter senses that, due to the use of specialist terminology, the message is not getting through, he/she can alert the professional to that fact and leave it up to him/her to deal with the problem. Interpreters are language experts not medical, legal, educational, welfare, political etc. experts. Explaining specialist terminology is the job of the professional, not the interpreter.

In the first instance, *accuracy* consists of not leaving parts of the meaning of an utterance out and of not adding anything to that meaning. That is, the interpreter must transfer exactly the same amount of information as is stated by the each interlocutor. If an utterance contains one point, that is all that must be conveyed. If it contains a point plus a clarification, both need to be conveyed. If an utterance contains an example illustrating a particular point, that example also needs to be conveyed. And if an utterance contains an offensive term or something that may cause insult, that, too, must be conveyed.

The interpreter does not act as a censor. It is the responsibility of the other parties to choose to put things in a particular way and, if they make unfortunate or inappropriate choices, it is they who must be held responsible for any consequences of communication breakdown. Unfortunately, it is often the case, especially in political and legal interpreting situations, that interlocutors do not accept this responsibility and instead blame the interpreter even though the interpretation was accurate.

Such inappropriate choices may be due to ignorance, carelessness, a conflict of expectations from the other parties or simply thinking of the interpreter as a filter who will make the utterance come out right anyway. Although the interpreter must avoid at all costs assuming such a 'filter' role, he/she may provide information of a cultural nature to enable the other parties to formulate their utterances so as to get the maximum benefit from the interpreted interview. If briefing has not been possible, for example, and if one of the parties uses a term the interpreter thinks may cause offence, the interpreter can simply ask that party, 'Do you wish me to interpret that?', thus giving that person the opportunity to think about what they are saying and leaving it to them to make the decision. Remember, however, that the other party has to be informed of what is happening. In this way the interpreter can help prevent an unpleasant situation.

Above all, the interpreter must take care not to say anything other than what the parties have said. Additions, suppressions, omissions and distortions all amount to inaccurate interpreting. If they occur, the interpreter is either linguistically and contextually not up to the task or may not be sure of how to apply language skills and other relevant knowledge. It is all a matter of training and practice. Training courses focus on these aspects intensively and attempt to make the students highly conscious of correct language usage and appropriate techniques in applying language and contextual knowledge. An accurate interpreter needs a high level of language skills and contextual knowledge as well as highly developed techniques (interpreting skills).

Accurate interpreting also entails *idiomatic usage* of language. This does not simply, as is often believed, consist of knowing the whole stock of idioms in both languages. Idiomatic language usage consists, above all, of using the appropriate forms (grammar, syntax, lexis, etc.) of a language as well as its collocations (which words may occur in constructions with which other words). Forms and collocations will vary from a little to a great deal across any two languages. An interpreter will sound most idiomatic when using forms and collocations appropriately (Larson, 1984: 141ff.). It is, of course, helpful to know as many idioms as one can manage in both languages. Idioms in one language often have equivalent counterparts in the other. Often, however, these counterparts express the same meaning by making reference to or using terms different from those used in the other language. The interpreter must be especially careful to ensure that he/she knows the real meaning of an idiom, in either language. To be near enough is not good enough. As for attempting to interpret idioms literally, in blind hope—the results are invariably hilarious.

Effective speaking skills, appropriate use of register, and accuracy in all its aspects make for *completeness* in the interpretation of the message. Of course, nuance and tone are often difficult to get across as they vary and are achieved through different means across languages. A supplementary explanation/clarification from the interpreter may sometimes be appropriate to complete the message, where even the best interpreting skills have come short of conveying nuance and tone.

Often *body language*–fidgeting, looks, nervous tics etc.–accompany a speaker's utterance and are part of the total message conveyed. Body language is often similar across cultures, so it does not need to be interpreted. There are, however, cases where not only is body language different across cultures but where people within one culture may express the same emotional state through a variety of body language. For example, some people will be very still when they're not sure they've understood something, while others will make that uncertainty very clear both through gestures and by asking questions. As in so many aspects of interpreting, assumptions are dangerous. If unsure, the interpreter must ask for explanations and clarifications in the way suggested above.

And if an interpreter is asked by one of the parties to interpret the other party's body language, the request must be politely but firmly refused. The onus must be put on the other parties to ask each other these questions. In debriefing, the interpreter may quite usefully give information about certain gestures and body language that are very clearly and universally acknowledged to mean something in a particular culture. But during the course of the interview, the interpreter must nip in the bud any attempts to engage the interpreter in any kind of activity that is not interpreting, such as consultation, explanation and clarification of a cultural nature etc.

The dynamics of liaison interpreting

Interviews involving interpreters can become very complex in terms of dynamics. Questions arise of who is conducting the interview, how the interview is conducted, who controls the flow of the communication etc. We must always remember that the objectives of an interview are not changed by the presence of an interpreter.

People often talk about the interpreter, the professional and the client as the participants in a bilingual interview. This approach is useful only up to a point. The basic model is of the professional interview, that is, the interaction between professional and client(s). While the presence of an interpreter does *not* change this basic interaction, it does influence the *way* in which the interview will be conducted.

From the point of view of the interpreter, it is better to talk about two clients. In other words, both the professional and the client are receiving the professional language services of the interpreter, because both have an equal need for these services. The original professional/client relationship is always there, but now another level of professional/client relationship is added—with the interpreter being the language professional having two clients. So a working model for an interpreted interview shows the basic direction of the flow of the communication as professional to client and client to professional, but conducted *via* the interpreter.

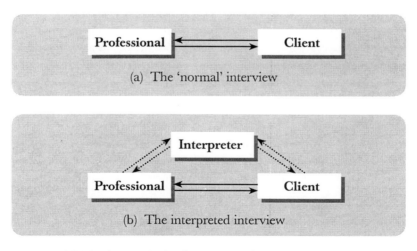

Models of communication flow in the professional/client interview

The professional '*controls*' the interview, that is, is responsible for what is said, how it is said, how questions are replied to etc. The only control the interpreter exercises is on the transfer of the message from one language system to another, that is, how best to convey the meanings of the professional and the client to enable the interview to achieve its objectives. The interpreter exercises the greatest control in this aspect when the messages come across the two languages accurately, completely, fluently, etc. Thus, the interpreter does not exercise control by telling the other parties what to do, in other words by changing the behaviour of the other parties. The most effective interpreter, the one who is most 'in control', is the one whose presence effects the least amount of disruption or change to the normal behaviour (linguistic and otherwise) of the other parties. It is usually interpreters who are not fully confident in their skills who will preface an interview by making requests of the other parties about how to speak and how much to say, and will even point out that they will 'interpret everything that is said'. What else is the interpreter there for, if not that?

The diagram indicates a three-way (three-cornered) communicative situation. This does not necessarily mean that there are always only three persons involved. It simply indicates that there are two languages involved with the interpreter being the channel via which the communication flows. Either language side can have any number of persons. There may even be a team of interpreters involved. Where there is one interpreter and a number of people involved on either language side, problems of interview management and crowd control can arise. Most of the time, however, these arise not because there is an interpreter present but because the dynamics of the situation have not been thought through by the other parties. If extensive briefing and preparation between the professional(s) and the interpreter(s) is possible, the communication dynamics and issues of control and management of the interview should be addressed.

It is the responsibility of the other professional(s) to determine how the interview needs to be conducted. Interpreters asked to interpret in a situation that is chaotic to begin with cannot be held responsible for any further chaos. An interpreter can only be held responsible for an interview breaking down if the interpretation itself has broken down.

The interpreter and cultural knowledge

People have often referred to interpreters as 'cultural bridges' or 'cultural brokers'. Such terms can have both positive and negative connotations. They do not mean that interpreters are somehow acting on behalf of other people or that they provide bridging mechanisms between people belonging to different cultures which go beyond the boundaries of bilingual communicative contexts as outlined. By the same token we must remember that language does not—and cannot—function outside context, cultural context and situational context (Halliday, 1981: 48), so the interpreter can make a legitimate cultural input.

The interpreter has knowledge of the cultures of both languages. The other parties may have knowledge of each other's cultures or they may not. The interpreter can make a contribution by explaining certain cultural aspects which may impinge on the interview at hand. This should only be done at the briefing stage in one-off situations and on a continuing basis where the interpreter is a regular member of a team of professionals—never in the course of an interview as an intervention. It can also be done at the debriefing stage to enable everybody to make fuller sense of what took place during the interview. Often participants have a feeling of uncertainty about what has been achieved, even when the interpreting is of top quality. This can be due to cultural factors, such as lack of knowledge, misunderstanding and conflict of expectations on either side. It is especially important for debriefing to take place in such situations, and it is appropriate for the interpreter to request such debriefing.

The interpreter must be extremely careful not to become an interpreter of cultural information in the other sense of the word, that is, not to step into the shoes of the other professional and attempt to use cultural knowledge to diagnose the situation. The interpreter can provide information of a cultural nature, but only the doctor, teacher, solicitor, social worker, businessman, etc. can make professional judgements and decisions using this information. Interpreters must, politely but firmly, stop attempts by other professionals to draw them into making other than linguistic and interpreting decisions.

Interpreters must also be careful not to promote cultural stereotypes in their giving of cultural information. Although certain general cultural characteristics will be true of all people of a particular culture, there is no such thing as a typical Greek, Arab, Chinese, Indonesian or any other nationality.

In summary:

- The *objectives* of an interpreted interview are *the same* as those of an interview not involving an interpreter, but the *dynamics* are *different*.
- It is important to have introductions, briefing and debriefing.
- Language skills are only one element of interpreting skills; a good interpreter must also have effective listening and speaking skills.
- Clarifications, explanations and interruptions may have a legitimate place in an interpreted situation, provided they are handled appropriately and strategically.
- An interpreter must not talk 'up' or 'down' to clients, and must not censor or summarise. Registers used by the interpreter's clients must be maintained by the interpreter.
- The interpreter's professional relationships are with two clients, who have a pre-existing and continuing professional relationship with one another. The interpreter's presence does not affect *what* takes place, it affects *how* the interview is conducted.
- The interpreter may provide information of a cultural nature to the clients provided that:
  - it is done appropriately, e.g. during briefing;
  - all parties are kept informed;
  - the interpreter is not put in a position of making decisions or judgments that belong to the *other* professional.

5 Ethics

All professions have to consider the question of ethics. In the vernacular, the adjectives 'professional' and 'ethical' are often synonymous, as are their opposites 'unprofessional' and 'unethical'. Among professionals and their clients, there is the perception that professionalism and ethics are inextricably linked, that you cannot claim to possess the former without also possessing the latter. Professional training courses usually include an ethics component, an admission that the possession of certain professional skills has to go hand in hand with some understanding of how to use those skills.

Definitions

Dictionary definitions of ethics go as follows: 'the science of morals', 'the rules of conduct recognized in certain limited departments of human life', 'the science of human duty in its widest extent' (*Oxford English Dictionary*), and 'the discipline dealing with what is good and bad or right and wrong or with moral duty and obligation', 'a group of moral principles or set values', 'a particular theory or system of moral values', 'the principles of conduct governing an individual or a profession', 'standards of behaviour' (*Webster's Dictionary*).

The link is between a way of conducting oneself as a professional and some moral considerations underlying such conduct. These moral considerations usually spring from a further underlying philosophical premise, containing two main considerations:

- Professionals supply a service for a fee, and the recipients expect an appropriate return for their money.
- The welfare of the recipients of many professional services is often in question, and this welfare necessitates ethical conduct. This is often defined as the 'service' orientation of professions: not only are they providing a particular item for money, but it is a service that affects basic aspects of the client's life—liberty, health. Indeed a client's welfare may be at stake directly or indirectly. For example, if a cabinet-maker makes a mess of renovating your kitchen, your pocket, peace of mind and routine will undoubtedly suffer, but probably not your long-term welfare. But if your doctor makes a wrong diagnosis, or a primary teacher fails to teach your child basic literacy skills, or your lawyer fails to do the necessary homework, then the long-term damage to your welfare will be more severe. We might classify the cabinet-maker's mess as having an *indirect* effect on your welfare, and the failings of the doctor, the teacher and the lawyer as having a *direct* effect on your welfare.

Liaison interpreting is a profession where, like medicine, teaching and the law, the client's welfare is usually affected *directly*. This is not only because most liaison interpreting takes place in the context of other professions such as medicine, teaching and the law, but also because interpreting has its own particular kinds of knowledge, skills and practices which require particular ethical considerations. Liaison interpreting is, then, subject to ethical considerations both along the lines of any other profession and along lines of its own. And because liaison interpreting takes place in the context of so many other professional and institutional settings, ethical conflicts often arise for the interpreter.

All professions share the basic philosophical premise that providing a service which affects the welfare of the client demands ethical practices. Every professional association sets up standards for its practitioners in order both to safeguard the welfare of its clients and to ensure that the professional activities of its members are of a high standard and that the profession has a high status in the eyes of society. These standards are called to question in cases of professional negligence or malpractice. Professions thus formulate codes of ethics which provide parameters within which professional decisions are made, parameters, that is, which act as rules of professional conduct. It is important to emphasize that these are parameters only, as no code of ethics can stipulate in a black and white fashion the dos and don'ts of any profession.

Every case of a professional/client consultation—doctor and patient, teacher and student, lawyer and client—has its own unique aspects and yet shares certain aspects with every other case. The professional is normally expected to exercise discretion in each case within the parameters provided by the code of ethics of that profession. When acting within these parameters a professional is acting professionally or ethically. When acting outside these parameters a professional is acting unprofessionally or unethically.

Liaison interpreting shares the general ethical considerations of all professions. At the same time, the nature of the knowledge and expertise that the liaison interpreter is expected to possess means that certain ethical considerations are peculiar to liaison interpreting.

General considerations

The most basic general considerations are confidentiality, impartiality and conflict of interest.

Confidentiality means that a professional must not disclose information about individuals or situations obtained in the course of professional duties unless permission has been granted by the persons involved or the professional is required to do so by anyone legally entitled to such information. Liaison interpreters must observe such confidentiality at all times.

Impartiality means that a professional must carry out professional duties to the best of his/her ability regardless of who the client is in terms of gender, race, social and economic status, ethnicity etc. The service provided must never be coloured by the professional's personal likes, dislikes, preferences, ideological leanings etc. Liaison interpreters must observe this principle also.

Conflict of interest concerns the professional's duty to act without regard to other interests such as personal or financial gain. Liaison interpreters are expected not to use information obtained from their clients for any external purpose.

Considerations peculiar to liaison interpreting

Some particular applications arise out of the very role of the interpreter. We have seen that the role of the interpreter is to facilitate communication in cases where the participants in an interview, ranging from a professional consultation to a business negotiation, do not speak the same language. We have also seen that the presence of an interpreter creates another level of professional relationships and dynamics in that the interpreter provides a professional language service to two or more clients.

In the course of the interpreting activity the interpreter usually becomes privy to *information of a non-linguistic nature*. In a medical situation the interpreter is privy to medical information about one of the clients, the patient. In a police interview the interpreter is privy to legal information about one of the clients, the interviewee. In a school situation the interpreter is privy to family information about one of the clients, the student or the student's family.

In all these situations, the information is the by-product of the professional interpreting function, and the interpreter is not the intended recipient of such information. The interpreter must maintain *confidentiality* about information that is the legitimate possession of the other professional and is the accidental or incidental possession of the interpreter. The interpreter must never use this incidental information for personal or financial gain or in any context where its use will create a *conflict of interest*.

Because of the variety of contexts in which liaison interpreting takes place, *issues of bias* of an ethnic, social, political, cultural or even gender nature can arise. For example, Arabic is the language of a great many different nationalities, and so is Spanish. Egyptians,

Lebanese, Syrians, Libyans etc. speak Arabic. Mexicans, Chileans, Colombians, Spaniards etc. speak Spanish. Yet, despite a common language, these national groups will exhibit an enormous variation of political, social, cultural etc. characteristics. It is not unusual for Arabic and Spanish interpreters to be asked by their clients where they come from, the subtext being 'Are you from my cultural group or another?' Clients may perceive this as important, and in some rare cases—for example, where a victim of political persecution encounters an interpreter from the cultural group that perpetrated that persecution—it must be treated as an issue, regardless of the politics or professionalism of that individual interpreter. On the whole, however, the professional liaison interpreter must behave impartially in regard to the ethnic, social, political etc. status of the clients. The interpreter who becomes aware of any interference in the interpreting task by such ethnic, social, political etc. issues, must refer those clients to another interpreter.

The liaison interpreter, as a facilitator of communication, offers *cultural expertise*. Indeed the interpreter cannot perform the linguistic part of interpreting without some relation to or some context of culture. One often hears such terms as 'cultural bridge' or 'cultural broker' used to describe the work or role of liaison interpreters. So cultural expertise related to both languages is an inextricable component of the interpreter's skills.

For example, a medical interpreter has knowledge not only of the patient's culture but also of the doctor's culture. This knowledge includes both formal aspects, such as how the profession is structured and conducts itself, and informal ones, such as patient expectations of a medical consultation. The professional interpreter uses such contextual knowledge to carry out the interpreting but not intervene in any other way.

It is not unusual for an interpreter to be asked in the course of an interpreted interview to make an assessment of a non-linguistic nature. A doctor, policeman, teacher etc. might ask the interpreter such things as: 'Do you think he's telling the truth?' 'Do you believe him?' These questions assume not only that the interpreter has the requisite professional knowledge to make such assessments but that it is a legitimate part of the role of interpreter to do so. Or a client may ask the interpreter to say whatever the interpreter thinks most likely to produce the result the client wants (for example in social security). This approach assumes that the interpreter is there to help the client's cause; it takes such a notion as 'cultural broker' to mean representing or acting on behalf of the client's interests.

The only ethical response to any such requests is to refuse them. This is not to say that the interpreter does not have a legitimate role in providing input of a cultural or professional nature. But this should happen in briefing and debriefing sessions or even as a continuing educational activity, and never in the course of an interview. Positive response to such requests will lead the interpreter into all sorts of complications and can even result in legal action for damages resulting from professional negligence or malpractice.

The question of *competence* is not generally an ethical issue but assumes ethical proportions in relation to liaison interpreting. Even when accreditation and registration mechanisms exist, the enormous variety of situations in which liaison interpreting takes place, as in Australia, means that there may be particular areas—both in terms of context and degree of specialization—where an accredited and registered interpreter may not have the requisite knowledge and skills to work effectively. Even the simplest interpreting situation requires linguistic, contextual and interpreting skills of the highest order. It is unethical to accept an assignment if the interpreter feels his/her skills are not adequate and there is not sufficient time to prepare. The best way out is to recommend a colleague whose skills are more suitable.

One exception to the general principles outlined is interpreting in *business situations*. The goal of a business negotiation is to strike a deal which is financially beneficial to each side. The ethics of doing business, in other words, are different from the ethics of practising medicine, law, teaching, social welfare etc. According to business ethics, an interpreter who is paid by a particular side in a business negotiation owes loyalty to that side. This means that the interpreter may have to do things like disclosing information and informing on colleagues' performance if these are considered to be of business advantage to the 'client'. In addition, the issues facing a staff interpreter differ from those faced by a freelance interpreter employed for a particular occasion. There is a situation of tension, in other words, between business ethics and professional ethics. An interpreter who objects in principle to such business practices should not accept interpreting assignments in the business context.

The fact that liaison interpreting, unlike other professional activities, is usually conducted in the context of other professional activities can lead to a tension similar to that in business—but for different reasons. We can understand this by referring to the role of the interpreter as a facilitator of communication between other professionals and their clients. A medical interview has the objective of diagnosing and treating a medical condition. A parent/teacher interview has the aim of identifying and solving problems of an educational and welfare nature in relation to the student. And a social worker/social benefits applicant interview has the objective of establishing eligibility criteria for the applicant. Any interpreting must give due consideration to the objectives of each situation. Such interviews take place in institutional settings and the interpreter often experiences tension between the institutional ethics of that setting and the ethics of interpreting.

In different *institutional settings*, relations with clients may demand quite different approaches. For example, in legal settings the adversarial system requires interpreters generally to avoid contact with any parties on the 'other' side—for example, a witness that the client will be referring to. This can mean physically ignoring their presence while waiting in a small ante-room for court proceedings to commence. The concern is one of possible collusion or an unfair attempt to influence a witness. On the other hand, an interpreter will often be a social 'ice-breaker', and getting to know the other party and the other party's interpreter may be a legitimate requirement of an interpreter. An interpreter who shuns such contact and restricts themselves strictly to interpreting may be doing less than their full job. Similarly, a hospital interpreter will often spend time with clients, familiarize themselves with the case, and, as part of a hospital organization, may well, for example, attend case conferences or physically guide the patient around a hospital. In the institutional setting of the hospital, patients' care is the first priority for all health workers. Thus in each of these institutional settings an interpreter will be behaving fully professionally while doing things that could not be contemplated in another of these settings.

In summary, interpreters, because the service they provide for a fee may directly affect the client's welfare, are subject to the same ethical principles as are all other professionals.

The following considerations are peculiar to liasion interpreting:

- 'Cultural expertise' may only be used to achieve effective interpreting, never to assume *another* professional role.
- It is unprofessional/unethical for an interpreter to accept work that is beyond his/her skills.
- When working in institutions which have specific ethical imperatives and objectives, interpreters will be governed by their own professional ethics and by the respective institutional ethics.
- Particular ethical considerations apply to liaison interpreting in business settings.

6 Professional Socialization

Professional socialization is the process by which a practitioner acquires the values and the behavioural patterns necessary to operate as a fully fledged member of a particular profession. It is important to specify some of these issues for liaison interpreting, precisely because of the stage of development at which the profession finds itself.

In the case of established professions, mechanisms have been developed whereby the new members of the profession are socialized. These include the identification of a well defined set of skills which characterizes the profession, the manner and means by which the profession is recognized by other professions and the public at large, training programmes, and the practice imperatives whereby professional conduct is integrated with the *modus operandi* of the organization(s) in which or for whom the work is carried out. This chapter will examine these elements as they apply to liaison interpreting.

In recent years a greater preoccupation with professionalism has, not surprisingly, coincided with an increase in demand for the services of liaison interpreters. More countries have been faced with mass influxes of people, and the acquisition of some political power by these groups has resulted in governments turning their minds to language services. Other branches of the interpreting profession have undergone different kinds of development at different times and have made greater strides in the area of professional socialization. Conference interpreting, for example, has had the organization of a professional grouping for almost five decades, while court interpreting has established a professional grouping in some countries and not others in relatively recent times. Other groupings such as interpreters for the media may alter the professional interpreting map of the future.

The profession of liaison interpreting finds expression in a number of ways depending on the social and cultural factors in particular countries. This is reflected in the variety of labels used for this type of interpreting around the world. Some examples are: community interpreting, ad hoc interpreting, contact interpreting, dialogue interpreting, three-cornered interpreting, public service interpreting, business negotiation interpreting. In relation to conference interpreting, and indeed any other kind of interpreting, liaison interpreting forms part of a continuum. The core practice and professional conduct parameters do not change, but the contexts in which the interpreting is performed demand particular responses and require the accentuation of certain aspects of professional practice and the attenuation of others.

Skills required

Any profession requires the gaining of competencies characteristic of the profession by the expenditure of considerable time and effort and, most importantly, the exercise of independent judgement and the acceptance of full responsibility for the quality and consequences of that judgement.

Which skills or competencies of the liaison interpreter qualify as professional skills? Clients would nominate *language skills*. The popular picture of the interpreter is of a polyglot who is also an automatic language converter: press the button and this person will convert your words from one language to another! Clearly, a gulf exists between reality and the perception of the interpreter's clients.

Language is of course the main component of the core skills of an interpreter. But what does *language competence* signify in this context?

It goes without saying that the liaison interpreter must have a command of at least two languages, in terms of their structure, usage and expressive potential. But this kind of language competence, while necessary, is not sufficient in itself. Indeed it can be achieved by any bilingual person. It is the utilization of this passive skill which begins to distinguish the bilingual person from the interpreter.

Language competence for the liaison interpreter, then, only begins with the kind of competence described above and then proceeds to other elements such as 'transfer' competence (Wilss, 1982):

- ability to produce a variety of synonymous or analogous expressions in both languages;
- ability to capture and reproduce register variations;
- ability to recognize and reproduce domain-specific expressions in a form which will be regarded as 'natural' by the respective users;
- ability to combine verbal and non-verbal communication cues from the source language and reproduce them in appropriate combinations in the target language;
- ability to identify and exploit rhythm and tone patterns of the languages in order to determine and utilize the 'chunks' of speech so as to maximize the efficiency of the interpreting;
- ability to speedily analyse the utterance in the context of the communication in order to anticipate the direction in which the argument is proceeding and the strategy being used in developing the argument.

A second component of interpreting skills is a group of elements defined as *cultural competence*. This group includes the possession of knowledge which enables the interpreter to comprehend the totality of the communicative intent of the speaker. This competence relates not so much to language as to the totality of the cognitive baggage which leads the speaker to produce the utterances. It involves recognition of any culturally determined assumptions implicit in the linguistic garb in which the audible and visible manifestation of the utterances is clothed. It relates to extra-linguistic knowledge about the world of the respective speakers, and is acquired through knowledge of social conventions, institutional practices, taboos, anthropologically and historically relevant elements of the cultures, and any sources from which speakers may draw inspiration for allusions and metaphoric constructions.

A third component is the group of elements properly considered *appropriate techniques* in the performance of the interpreting task. These include knowledge of the dynamics of communication, which allows the interpreter to consider such aspects as:

- the spatial arrangements between the participants;
- techniques for dealing with aspects of control of the situation (including techniques for interrupting the speaker or ensuring that only one speaker intervenes at a time);
- techniques which utilize knowledge of group dynamics for the identification of the different roles being played by each of the clients;
- techniques more specifically directed at the interpreting output itself, such as note-taking;
- techniques for ordering information input so as to minimize the likelihood of omissions;
- techniques related to voice production and modulation in order to make the interpretation audible, clear and unambiguous;
- techniques to minimize the difference between an interpreted interview and an interview where an interpreter is not required— such as the control of the speed of the interpretation to minimize the time taken, control of the congruence of the tone of voice due to the emotional charge of the utterance and that of the interpretation of the utterance, handling of repetitions on the part of the speaker and the whole issue of redundancy in speech.

A fourth component, which is often the subject of heated debate, is *the question of memory* and its role in consecutive interpreting, of which liaison interpreting is a manifestation. This issue is complicated by the fact that it is difficult to attribute breakdowns in interpreting performance to problems of memory, even though novice interpreters believe this is often the case. It is not clear whether memory is simply the ability to recall with a high degree of accuracy what the speaker has said, or whether the causes of such breakdowns are due to problems of comprehension in the first place because of a lack of ability to connect the utterances into a meaningful message. Much more research is required before definitive comments can be made about this phenomenon. Given the possibility of note-taking in the vast majority of assignments, it is perhaps more fruitful to look to the relationship between comprehension and interpreted output rather than memory alone.

The last component can be subsumed under the rubric of *professional competence* and includes such competencies as the ability to make independent judgements in terms of the linguistic, ethical, socio-cultural and affective issues which arise in an interpreted situation and in relations with colleagues and other professional groups.

The fundamental skill is the ability to maintain a clear focus on the interpreter's role as an abstract construct, while evaluating each situation and issue and making decisions which are consonant with that role but also take into account and cater for the singularity of each situation. The capacity to adapt to situations is a central attribute of the liaison interpreter. It imposes obligations on the interpreter to prepare for assignments by becoming familiar with the topic to be discussed; not only with its particular lexicon but, more importantly, with the characteristics of the discourse which is likely to be utilized.

A related issue is the question of *specialization*. It is well known that specialization exists in conference interpreting, and court interpreting could be regarded as a specialization. Specialization is related to market demands as much as to skills and it is most likely that different employment contexts will lead to different approaches in this area.

Recognition of the profession

An essential ingredient of professional socialization is the need for the skills and performance of liaison interpreters to be recognized and valued not only by clients but by the population at large. The main route to this recognition is through the quality of performance of the individual members of the profession; it is through their work and their ability to articulate the essence of their profession that this recognition is achieved.

Positive and clear steps can be taken in order to accelerate this process. One of these is the development of a strong professional body to propagate knowledge about the profession and to play a monitoring and gate-keeping role for admission to the profession, including establishing standards of performance and applying sanctions to those members who do not abide by them. Liaison interpreting is in a particularly vulnerable position in this respect. The profession relies on the collective performance of individuals and on feedback from clients who are qualified to assess only some aspects of the overall performance of the interpreter, which are perhaps not the central ones for the development of the profession.

In a global sense, the profession can only point to societal indicators to reflect the way it is viewed by the public. These include the status accorded to it, which manifests itself in the prevailing remuneration levels, the resources which the society is prepared to invest in the training of interpreters, and the systems set up for the control of access to the profession in terms of registration or licensing of practitioners.

In general, liaison interpreting has not fared too well if one judges it by the above indicators. The reasons are rooted in the fact that the work of the liaison interpreter is not public, in the sense that interpreters work alone and deal with private matters concerning few individuals at a time. In addition, the liaison interpreter often works in environments and with clients who do not possess the political power or prestige to influence and modify public opinion on the perceptions about the interpreter. The industrial power of the liaison interpreter is also limited in that, without controls on the entry to the profession, industrial action is ineffectual. Advances must be made, through the lengthy process of communication, in educating the public at large about the work of the liaison interpreter.

Training programmes

A major catalyst of professional socialization is a course of training which qualifies graduates for entry into the profession. Although this method of professional socialization is well accepted by the majority of professions, with interpreting, and liaison interpreting in particular, there is still some way to go. The reasons are varied and complex. On the one hand, the proponents of the 'innate skill' hypothesis regard the ability to perform interpreting tasks as an innate ability which some people possess and others don't. On the other hand, confusion in many people's minds about the relationship between language competence and interpreting competence leads to the attitude that language training by itself is sufficient to produce professional interpreters.

We regard neither of these approaches as considered responses. Implicit in the development of the professional liaison interpreter is the identification of a set of skills and attributes which leads to the formulation of a curriculum for the training of people who possess certain aptitudes. A training model is essential.

Discussion of the skills required by the liaison interpreter provides a blueprint for the consideration of training issues. *Distinction between language competence and interpreting competence* is the fundamental principle which informs the development of the curriculum—which in turn serves as an instrument of professional socialization. This distinction and the difficulties which arise in its implementation in the curriculum cannot be overemphasized. Interpreting training represents not work *on* language but work *with* language; just as it is problematic to pursue studies in physics without a knowledge of mathematics, so it is with interpreting and language.

The curriculum seeks to follow through all phases of the interpreting process and to expose the student not only to the practical and technical aspects of the profession but, in many ways more importantly, to invite *reflection on the principles and assumptions which inform the practice*. For this reason the preparation of an interpreter involves training *and* education. Training is often viewed in the narrow sense of imparting skills which will then be utilized in practice. But this model alone is not sufficient, since it is impossible in any course to achieve a complete coverage of the myriad potential interpreting situations. A capacity to adapt skills and make judgements about particular situations is essential. In other words, the work of the interpreter is *not* mechanical, and mechanical responses are inappropriate and lead to poor performance.

With the uninformed assumption that interpreting is about language rather than communication, the *non-language elements are often overlooked* or relegated to the status of electives. The danger is that graduates who see themselves as language experts will, once in the workforce, perpetuate the narrow view of the interpreter as a polyglot, and thus contribute very little to the process of professional socialization.

Tension exists between the interpreter's need to be global and to evaluate the total performance in an interpreting situation, and the curriculum as a sequence of educational objectives which necessitates breaking down the interpreting performance into pedagogically manageable portions. Universities tend to dissect curricula into identifiable and specifically named units, for administrative as well as pedagogic convenience. Often this produces dysfunction, and particularly careful and constant co-ordination is required between the elements of an interpreting course and the staff who teach them.

Programmes specifically for liaison interpreters are a very recent phenomenon, and in different parts of the world have been influenced by pre-existing conditions in the interpreting profession as a whole. The programmes are not always university courses; they range from short in-service programmes aimed at practitioners who are deemed not to have the professional skills, to postgraduate programmes.

The variation reflects the relative degree of importance accorded to liaison interpreting and the sequence in which interpreting developments have taken place. In general terms where conference interpreting courses were already established, liaison interpreter training tends to be non-existent or takes the form of employer-driven in-service programmes. Where the interpreting profession began with liaison interpreters, the courses tend to be conducted by universities. There are some hybrid systems where students may use different exit points during the course of undergraduate degrees depending on the type of interpreting they wish to undertake. Such systems do not generally specify exit points for liaison interpreting, except in some cases where 'business negotiation interpreter' is clearly indicated as an exit point.

By its very nature, liaison interpreting has had to deal with language combinations which are often not considered in the sphere of conference interpreting. The interactions tend to involve languages considered on a world scale as of 'limited diffusion'. This brings with it particular problems for training and general professional development—as discussed in Chapter 3.

Training programmes require a close relationship between the training institution and the field which employs the graduates, which is often manifested in extensive on-the-job practice as part of the training programme. This contributes to the solution of some of the problems related to role and professional socialization.

Practice imperatives

Apart from the development of skills, the recognition of the profession and the completion of training, the other element vital to professional socialization is the application of professional standards in practice.

In the initial period particularly, the practitioner is confronted with the exigencies and pressures which derive from institutional as well as professional considerations. The interpreter, in close contact with the clients, must deal with local versus general work rules which may impinge on the interpreting task but over which the interpreter may have no control. In particular, rules of behaviour laid down for the organization for good and proper reasons may contravene some aspect of the professional conduct of the interpreter. Typically this occurs in a service organization such as a counselling service where casual conversations with clients before a counselling session may be seen as beneficial and as contributing to the service provided. But this kind of interaction may pose problems to the interpreter who does not wish to run the risk of being told by that client during the counselling session that the information being sought has already been supplied in an informal encounter. Since the interpreter works alone, these discrepancies between what is required by the profession and what is understood and accepted by the work place can be a considerable source of distress. Training programmes must equip people to deal with these situations and resolve these dilemmas.

The tendency of employers to treat new graduates as fully established professionals is another source of difficulty. This stems in part from the general misconception that because interpreters control their own work, they are immune from the teething problems which all new graduates experience when integrating into any profession. This unrealistic expectation also contributes to the view that in-service training and development ought to concentrate on elements which have more to do with socialization into the institution than into the profession.

The relations of the interpreter with professionals in other fields merits some consideration. Such colleagues may well share general misconceptions and preconceived ideas about the nature and performance of the interpreter's work. In order to cultivate a comfortable and workable professional relationship with such colleagues, the interpreter must assume the role of educator. The interpreter must communicate in a direct and well argued fashion the parameters of performance of the interpreting function, and influence any other professionals to modify their behaviour in order to cater for those elements of interpreting practice which are not negotiable. This task is not required of those within more established professions whose function is widely understood and accepted by the wider community.

In summary, the four main elements of professional socialization for liaison interpreters—a well defined set of skills, recognition of the profession, training and practice imperatives—are still problematic. They require careful consideration by the practitioners, employers and educators alike if there is to be progress in the understanding and acceptance of the liaison interpreter.

Specialist Areas of Work

The previous chapters have established a set of theoretical and practical perspectives which define the basis of the liaison interpreter's role, and illustrate in very general ways how the interpreter should, and should not, operate.

Generally speaking, the settings in which liaison interpreting occurs have fundamentally similar discourse structures, with the greatest variation being in specialized terminology. Interviews with a local government official, a doctor or a lawyer, or a meeting between two businessmen, may differ greatly in terminology, and knowledge of that terminology and of procedures and context are necessary prerequisites for professional interpreting. But the techniques used by the interpreter, the role the interpreter plays and the status of the communicated message in these commonest situations may not differ greatly.

However, even within the typical bureaucratic, medical or legal spheres, particular situations may not fit this simple pattern of relying only upon straightforward techniques. In such situations the purpose of interchange is usually not merely, or primarily, communication as normally understood. The intention of communication may be specifically forensic, or symptomatic, or a particular communication may deliberately or unintentionally carry meta-linguistic connotations that fundamentally alter the nature of the communication—as in these examples:

- A psychiatrist interviewing a patient, while interested in the narrative account of a particular incident, may be very much more interested in the style of expression, exact words and images used, repetitions and elisions, stress patterns. The interview may be a vehicle for coming to important conclusions about the patient *on the basis of the patient's pattern of communication.* The patient, of course, is likely to come to a conclusion about the psychiatrist on similar grounds.
- In speech therapy, the style and detail of the communication again becomes the 'content' of any message. The interpreter must attend to many detailed aspects of actual speech that would be unimportant in other settings, and almost inevitably must give *descriptions* of the communication pattern.

- In court-room cross examination, lawyers and witnesses may use word-plays to attack and defend. And, as the demeanour of a witness may be crucial for issues of credibility, the problem arises of how to convey demeanour via verbal interpretation.
- The demeanour of the participants may also be important in business negotiations. As each party may have their own staff interpreter, the role of the interpreter subtly shifts to that of a member of a team rather than a neutral facilitator—the interpreter being listened to by the other party for tactical clues.
- Counsellors may use subtle forms of communication—for example, by refusing to 'understand' what the client is saying, with the object of eliciting more information or enabling assessment of the situation.

In these situations and many more, *the communication process itself has particular status*. The 'message' in narrative or experiential terms is not the whole object of interaction nor necessarily the substantial part of what is communicated. Such situations require a more theoretical and questioning stance towards the role of the interpreter in transferring a message. When the status of the message is itself of prime interest to one or both parties, the interpreter must be aware of the context and status of the message, as this may affect both technique and role in conveying the full ambit of the communication.

We will now look at four fields where understanding the peculiar nature of communication (and mis-communication) are vital to the successful performance of interpreting: mental health, the law, business and speech pathology.

7 Mental Health

We shall leave to one side those aspects of psychiatric or mental health work that create difficulties for all mental health workers: the milieu of mental health settings (e.g. psychiatric hospitals); disconcerting, strange or threatening behaviour. While these affect the interpreter's work and need to be understood, they are general issues faced by any mental health worker.

The issues peculiar to interpreters have to do with the *nature of communication* in mental health settings. First, interpreters must understand the *purposes* of psychiatric interviewing and therapy sessions, and the role communication plays within them. Secondly, psychiatric interviews will often be characterized by *distortions* to 'normal' communication patterns, which are vital for diagnosis and treatment but which present numerous problems of technique for interpreters.

Purposes of the psychiatric interview

At the most basic level, many psychiatric interviews will differ little from ordinary medical interviews:

- Have you been taking your tablets?
- Are you sleeping well?

And these questions may receive brief answers that present no unusual problems for the interpreter. However, even for these simple questions, the psychiatrist may be more interested in the patient's *reactions*, rather than the formal answer. The interpreter will need to develop a technique to convey the exact and full nature of the patient's response to these questions—be it one of spontaneity, dullness, anxiety and so forth.

But beyond this simple level of questioning, interviews may probe deeply into a patient's experiences and feelings. This raises important issues of understanding and technique for the interpreter. There is a range of views within the psychiatric profession itself over the purposes and techniques of psychiatric interview. One of the more comprehensive approaches is exemplified by the American psychiatrist Harry Stack Sullivan's now classic definition of the psychiatric interview:

> such an interview is a situation of primarily *vocal* communication in a two-group, more or less *voluntarily integrated*, on a progressively unfolding *expert–client* basis for the purpose of eliciting *characteristic patterns of living* of the subject person, the patient or client, which patterns he experiences as particularly troublesome or especially valuable, and in the revealing of which he expects to derive *benefit*. (Sullivan,1954: 4)

Note, to begin with, that the emphasis is not on verbal but on *vocal communication*, posing the first challenge for the interpreter. This attention to the vocal demands that the interpreter reflect not only *tone* (loudness, rapidity, excitedness, passiveness), but also the more particular vocal indicators of *demeanour* (precise manner of speech, whether clipped, hesitant, forceful etc.), much of which might not be conveyed to the psychiatrist purely by auditory cues.

Beyond this, and fundamental to the psychiatric process, is the ability to understand the *interplay of verbal and vocal* factors, as this transcript from a British patient/psychiatrist interview shows:

> Patient: You are just sitting there, I know . . . You are going to do just the same as everyone else. You don't want to help me. You think that I am incurable. They all say that. They listen to me very politely, just like you, and then they show me the door. They think I am violent. I AM NOT A VIOLENT MAN. I have insight into my problems,

> but nobody believes me. YOU DON'T BELIEVE ME DO YOU? You think I need pills. They all want me to take pills. I am not going to take pills. I AM NOT GOING TO TAKE PILLS. That's what you want, isn't it? You would like to send me away to someone who will just give me pills. I may have violent phantasies, but that is different. I AM NOT A VIOLENT MAN. No-one believes me when I try to tell them that. (Casement, 1985: 146)

The vocal aspects must be attended to because a psychiatrist who does not share the patient's language cannot easily make judgements about the patient's vocal features unless they are conveyed exactly by the interpreter. Languages and cultures do differ in many vocal aspects such as loudness or forcefulness, or how anger or politeness are expressed.

And, at a further level still, the interpreter will be involved in *communicative therapy*, that is, a therapy in which communication with the patient is either a total or substantial part of the process of therapy itself (as opposed, say, to a therapy consisting only of chemical treatment in which communication cues are relevant only to diagnosis and monitoring of progress). In such situations, the communicative pattern of the psychiatrist must be conveyed as accurately as that of the patient. For some therapies which seek to recreate feelings, precise vocal cues are of the utmost importance, as in this extract from a Gestalt therapy group session recorded by J. K. Zweig of the analyst Lankton's work:

Lankton: (Finishing with another client) Now Violet, what are you experiencing (actually turning and sitting like Violet is sitting; legs crossed, palms up on lap, head erect, and lips together without a smile)?

Violet: (Jerks back as she notices him) I didn't know it was my turn to work (sarcastic tone of voice).

Lankton: (With sarcastic voice, like hers) You never know what you will experience, until you make yourself available for new experience.

Violet: (Pupils dilate, face muscles flatten, blink slows, respiration slows. She nods her head slowly, as if to show agreement.)

Lankton: (Waits, still matching her behaviour).

Violet: I feel crowded!

Lankton: And how is it for you to feel crowded? Give yourself room to experience being crowded (pauses) and put words to it.

Violet: (Defocuses her eyes and stares, changes posture as she pulls her legs to her chin and entwines her arms around her legs).

Lankton: Stay there—with yourself and come to know where you are crowded. (Leans forward but does not further match her specific behaviour).

Violet: (Closes her eyes) I'm crowded in, closed in.

Lankton: What do you experience enclosing you?

Violet: I'm in a box. Now I feel like I was (voice gets more faint) just too little. (Begins to cry as her face muscles lose all tonus and pallor increases)

Lankton: (Changes voice to a softer, melodic tone) Say that in the present tense—'I am just too little'.

Violet: (Haltingly at first) I . . . I'm just too little . . . I can't push it . . . can't push the . . . (changes to original voice tone) I don't know what I'm talking about.

Lankton: (Changes to original tone of voice) You have some unfinished business back there. You will know where after you experience it. Perhaps the safety in this room releases you to find out what you will find.

Violet: I don't know . . . (pauses, moves her eyes up to the left and then she begins to stare ahead) . . . I'm too big to fit in here. I can pull my legs up like this. This refrigerator is big, bigger than those boxes. It opens really hard, makes a funny noise. I like it. (It) feels smooth inside. There is not as much room in here as I thought there was. (Pauses) I could go to sleep in here. The door is closed and it's dark, really dark. I don't think I want to be in here any more. The door won't open—I can't get out, I can't get out . . .

Lankton: Make noise!

Violet: Ahh, Mommy, I can't get out, can't get out, let me . . . HELLLLLPP (cries and leaps from chair)

Lankton: You're out! (holding her) Can you finish this situation by being here and being free?

Violet: I'm scared. I'm right here, hanging on tight (to therapist's hand).

> Lankton: How are you scaring yourself? There is nothing scary here.
> Violet: (Standing and speaking to the group with a growing smile) I made noise when I was scared. I got out of there. I moved. I thought. I thought about what I needed even when I was scared. That was a good decision. Guess that was what I did (sits down and begins recovering from the unexpected incident). (Zweig, 1982: 139)

Zweig tells us that the patient had been locked in a refrigerator at the age of two, an incident of which she had no conscious memory.

Note the range of vocal and verbal features employed by both psychiatrist and patient. Such features also come up in related therapies, including hypnosis. If patients who do not speak the language of the therapist are to have access to such therapies, interpreters will need to be used, and the interpreter thus needs to understand the purpose of various psychiatric encounters, and the centrality of communication in these processes.

Patients will have their own purposes in psychiatric interviews. Interpreters will encounter exchanges where statements may be pointedly communicating a patient's needs or wishes to the therapist—pauses are used as cues, and shifts in discourse are strategically important for the patient, as in this British example:

> Patient: I cannot stand the pressures at work. I think I may have to find another job.
> Therapist: Have you ever thought of going to a careers advice centre?
> Patient: I was thinking about that myself, but I don't think I should need to be given advice about what to do with my life. I ought to be able to get in touch with that within myself. (Pause) I only came back to London after the summer holiday because of you, but I now feel angry with you for some reason. (Pause) My boss will be back tomorrow. I know what it will be like: he will be constantly telling me what to do—interfering pressure all the time. He never seems to see me as being able to do things for myself. (Casement, 1985: 186)

The exactness of tone, emphasis and fidelity to pauses and pointedness of comment are crucial here in the conveying of cues.

Pauses are particularly difficult. The British playwright Harold Pinter is well known for his detailed indications of pauses in his scripts, and his exhaustive discussions with directors on their use. For Pinter, pauses indicate crucial moments in the dramatic action; their role in the dialogue above is no less crucial.

Two points of technique can already be drawn from these examples. First, *the interpreter must convey the full range of vocal and verbal behaviour* of the participants, upon which diagnosis and treatment will depend. Secondly, because the discourse may be emotionally charged and completely engrossing to the person communicating, *interruption may be difficult.*

Some of the normal conventions of turn-taking, question/answer, or signalling to one of the parties to stop to allow interpretation (when the interpreter's memory is stretched to the limit) may fly out the window. A patient may recount an incident in an engrossed manner for several minutes, or it may be clear that any interruption would destroy a particular train of thought or action. The interpreter needs a technique to cope with this. Normally, note-taking is taboo in psychiatric cases. The usual recourse is either to simultaneous interpreting, to a method of interruption and turn-taking that is not totally destructive of the intention to continuing communication, or to development of a highly capable memory. A combination of all three is sometimes required.

Even for the most skilled interpreter, there may be features of utterances that cannot be rendered into the other language, particularly where the utterance is highly distorted, or physical and vocal features are overwhelming. But even in the simplest psychiatric encounter, an interpreter will have to *describe* a feature of a patient's communication which cannot be rendered into the other language. For example, excessive or heavy breathing which interferes with word and sentence formation may be almost impossible to render in the other language, but a description of it will give data for diagnosis or response by the psychiatrist. And a patient's pauses must be conveyed convincingly, and not mistaken for the interpreter searching for a word—again, a description of the communication can be given.

Distorted communication

The next set of issues relates to the problems of communication itself in mental health settings.

In a situation of extreme stress and perhaps some thought confusion, the discourse may be incoherent, fragmented, jumping from issue to issue, as in this short sample:

> Patient: Yoga . . . (Pause) Falling . . . everything falling . . . no stopping (Pause) Being held . . . Yoga teacher holding me . . . Pause) In pieces . . . They wrote to me . . . The Yoga class . . . (Pause) Six months since . . . hadn't been since . . . I'm falling again . . . I can't stop the falling. (Casement, 1985: 149)

Disconnected (or seemingly disconnected) discourse is most difficult for any listener to remember clearly and reproduce. For example, everyone has more difficulty in remembering lists of nonsense syllables than real words, or lists of unconnected words than patterns of words, as in poetry. Furthermore, in a psychiatric setting perfectly smooth and 'normal' discourse may be suddenly punctuated with a seemingly irrelevant but important and revealing aside, or a complete reorientation of discourse. This may be occasional, or signal a progressive turn of the discourse towards psychotic discourse, as illustrated in Bent Rosenbaum and Harley Sonne's Scandinavian example:

> I[nterviewer]: Why is this a good day to die?
> P[atient]: Because today I feel that I have achieved something which I have . . . I have thought for many years that I would like to exp–to try to experience.
> I: And what is that?
> P: To be a media object.
> I: Has that been a great wish of yours?
> P: It has, actually, for a very long time, so that's why I'm completely cul–curazy with delight; also because of the cigarette, however, I must admit.
> I: That's also 'to be a media object,' of course?
> P: Well, that depends on the way you look when you smoke; you see,

> if I sit shaking then it will have a deterrent effect. Because I, um, I am using the cigarette once too often and end up doing something like this, which I will never dare to do again. It simply hurt so terribly that I got my threshold of pain raised. Because that one is the first, that those are some of the other . . . things up there, and I did this simply in a rage at a conference. [The patient indicates a line of scars from burns produced by lighted cigarettes.]
>
> I: Hm. Are you often in a rage?
>
> P: Um, I don't understand that. Are you being rude? I believe I am being used as light [. . .] (Rosenbaum and Sonne, 1986: 58)

This kind of discourse can also characterize the recounting of dreams.

At perhaps the deepest level, the language of *psychosis* taxes the interpreter with a seeming swirl of shotgun-scattered references and continual elaborations and jumps in reference. Rosenbaum and Sonne's revealing transcripts include some patient-constructed *neologisms*, these deriving from Nordic mythology and fable:

> P[atient]: And after all there are . . . but there the state has done very good work, they have discovered the hundred thousand million times million three hundred things on the bottom of the Silkeborg Lakes. Crimes happen all the time on the bottom of the Silkeborg Lakes, in the Zealand Lakes and the North Sea, and up in the rainbows, they had looked up into the clouds, put into the mannequins, yes, there . . . down in, down in caves, all possible places.
>
> I[nterviewer]: Has the state done all that?
>
> P: No, those who are interfering.
>
> I: Aha.
>
> P: But, uhm, nobody is allowed except trisks and svilts.
>
> I: No.
>
> P: But now . . . under Øste Søgade [a street in Copenhagen], there they have beated three hundred, eight, eight thousand, um, three hundred things, or one hundred, three hundred things down with sexual . . . big sexual organs, so that liver, kidney, and lungs slide out crushed. One can see down there, they are carried up day and night. And it's like that all over the country on all plan . . . thirty planets they have done the same. (Rosenbaum and Sonne, 1986: 80)

Just how important the accurate rendition of such a stream of discourse can be is evident from the authors' analysis of the chain of reasoning that they see in this text, and which will certainly not be apparent at first reading. An interpreter, of course, hears it only *once*. (Ibid.: 82)

The reference to 'trisks and svilts' relates to use of Nordic mythology by the patient elsewhere in the interview. As the psychiatrist will not of course be of the same cultural background as the patient, the interpreter's ability to render such references becomes an important asset. Those neologisms which cannot be rendered clearly into the other language must be described adequately so that their features are understood.

Conveying systematic distortions of communication thus takes on a particular importance in mental health interpreting because of the use of this data in diagnosis and therapy (and, of course, particular vocal features of the therapist's reaction must also be conveyed). Even the smallest details of communication style must be faithfully transmitted: for example, stuttering, slurring and vocal peculiarities of any kind. Slips of the tongue, which are seen as important in some schools of psychiatry, also fall into this category. While some interpreters will in any situation deliver such slips in an exact manner, in a psychiatric situation they may have a particular status for diagnosis. The American psychiatrist John Thompson recounts an interview with a patient who came to him, five months pregnant, having left college and not wanting to get married:

> I asked her if she had informed the father of the baby, whom she had not seen for four months, of her pregnancy. 'Yes,' she said, 'I did drop him a little note to let him know that our relationship was the product of a child'. (Thompson, 1987: 150)

In summary, certain base rules must be followed by interpreters in mental health situations:

- The interpreting must give exact renditions of both vocal effects and content, or confess them unrenderable and describe their communicative features.

- To make chunks of dialogue manageable, interpreters must be able to work simultaneously on occasion, or to develop exceptional memory, or to develop an acceptable intervention technique.
- Interpreters can expect to be asked about cultural references that seemingly can make no sense to a listener from another culture.
- Interpreters must not make or attempt diagnosis. More subtly, they must not make 'interpretations' of what the patient *means*, as meaning here is the outcome of analysis of primary data—principally verbal and vocal communication. The interpreter is concerned solely with conveying that data into the other language.
- Recounting must be in the first person. (Interestingly, while all interpreters agree on the necessity to use the first person when conveying what the patient says, some tend to use the third person to convey what the doctor says, in an attempt to avoid confusion in the patient as to who is giving orders/instructions/questions.)
- Interpreters may be involved in a team approach, and attend case conferences and the like where their interpreting and language expertise can be valuable in assessment and treatment.

The story is told, unfortunately not apocryphally, of the interpreter coming into a psychiatric interview where the following communication took place:

Patient:	(any of the patient texts reproduced above)
Interpreter:	(long, long pause)
Psychiatrist:	(finally) What did they say?
Interpreter:	I don't know, they're mad!

The interpreter must have a clear understanding of the main approaches and methodologies of psychiatry, the likely situations to be encountered and, above all, the role of communication itself in both diagnosis and therapy. For an interpreter thus equipped, the mental health field becomes not only one of the most challenging but also one of the most satisfying.

8 Legal Settings

The previous chapter highlights the special issues facing interpreters in mental health settings: the central role that communication plays in the purposes of psychiatric interviews and the departures from 'normal' communication patterns. To some extent, the same can be said about legal interpreting. Communication plays a crucial role in achieving the goals of the legal system, and distortions to normal communication patterns do occur. For example, court-room communication patterns differ from those of everyday discourse because of the need to conform to strict legalistic constraints (Conley and O'Barr, 1990: 12–15)

However, there are significant differences. First, whereas in mental health settings, different types of discourse derive from the psyche of the patient (i.e. disconnected discourse is produced by people in certain states of mind), in legal settings other factors—mostly external to the speakers—give rise to different types of discourse. Secondly, the causes of distortions to 'normal' communication patterns are different and, unless recognized and dealt with appropriately by interpreters, can have a profound impact on the parties involved. Thirdly, whereas psychiatry is grounded in a scientific field, the legal system is a social institution generally committed to the notions of fairness and equity and to longstanding traditions; underlying tensions stemming from these commitments may present dilemmas of role for interpreters.

We define legal interpreting as a service rendered strictly within the operation of the legal system, the content of which is substantially legal in nature. Thus interpreting for a medical consultation associated with a legal case is not viewed as legal interpreting, but interpreting for a lawyer/client conference is.

This chapter contains:

- description of the work of legal interpreters;
- critical analysis of the demands that the legal system places on interpreters;
- examination of a number of specific issues, including the impact of interpreter performance on the communication dynamics of a cross-examination.

Note that the word 'English' represents the mainstream language of the society.

LEGAL INTERPRETING IN OPERATION

Legal interpreting covers a multitude of situations—too many to describe. Instead, we will describe the interpreting assignments arising out of a criminal case. It is not meant to be taken as a typical case, as there are many different mechanisms for dealing with such cases. However, the principles and issues pertaining to interpreting that this case raises are essentially the same as in other cases (Driesen, 1988).

This case begins with the arrest of the suspect, followed by his interview at a police station. The police lay charges against him at a local court in front of a magistrate who grants the suspect bail. The accused receives legal advice from a solicitor who then represents him at his committal or preliminary hearing, as required by the particular legal system. A plea of not guilty is entered and the case proceeds to a trial by jury.

Throughout this process, interpreters are called upon:

- in the police interview;
- in the local court when the charges are laid and bail application is heard;

- for lawyer/client conferences;
- in court during the committal hearing and the trial, both for witnesses giving evidence-in-chief and being cross-examined and re-examined, and for the accused to enable him to follow the proceedings.

Police interviews

Most interpreting assignments of this type take place at a police station. The interviewee may be a witness or a suspect. The interpreter may be called at unusual hours of the day with minimum notice. The atmosphere at a police station is cold and impersonal, some would say intimidating. Often the non-English speaking (NES) client is shocked, frightened and disoriented, leading to identification with the interpreter who is often the only participant from the same background. This identification sometimes leads to the NES client trying to converse with or elicit advice from the interpreter. Understandable as it may be, if not dealt with in an appropriate manner this can result in the English speaking clients feeling left out or, even worse, suspicious of collusion between the interpreter and the NES client.

Generally speaking, the interpreter's role is straightforward and readily understood by all sides. However, police interviews have a number of distinctive formal and environmental features:

- Warnings or injunctions may need to be given (e.g. warnings on rights or obligations) which are formally essential to the interview and their status needs to be clearly conveyed.
- In many jurisdictions, accused or others have the right to silence, and the presence of the interpreter must not interfere with or influence in any way the exercise of this right.
- These interviews may involve substantial amounts of sight translation, e.g. of transcripts of interview or other documents.
- They may be required by law to be audio-taped or video-taped. In increasing numbers of jurisdictions, for indictable matters, all interviews of suspects must be audio-taped or the evidence collected could be inadmissible at a court hearing. A copy of the

tape-recording, together with its transcript where applicable, must be given to the interviewee or his/her lawyer.
- The police interview often forms the basis upon which a suspect is charged, and very often is the crucial evidence that would determine the outcome of the case (Willis and Sallman, 1984: 47).

During the interview, a police officer asks questions in English, the interpreter conveys the questions into the other language, the accused answers in that language and the interpreter conveys the answers into English. The English part of this bilingual exchange is typed up and becomes the record of interview.

The following excerpt from a police record of interview illustrates the kind of content, both in terms of subject matter and language used, that an interpreter can expect:

Police record of interview

    Police officer: You understand that I wish to speak to you in relation to an incident that occurred at the Coroner's Court earlier today?
    Interviewee: Can you tell me with—why I give an answer in court? What's wrong with them? Why a—this time I still have to be here?
    Police officer: Well, before I go into that I must inform you that you are not obliged to say or do anything, but anything you say or do may be given in evidence. Do you understand that?
    Interviewee: Understand.
    Police officer: I must also inform you of the following rights: you may communicate with, or attempt to communicate with, a friend or relative to inform that person of your whereabouts; and you may communicate with, or attempt to communicate with, a legal practitioner. Do you understand those rights?
    Interviewee: Understand.
    Police officer: Do you wish to do either of those things?
    Interviewee: Yes.
    Police officer: What does he wish to do?
    Interviewee: I want to let my relative know that I'm here.
    Police officer: A'right. Well, before we do that, I'll just—I'll just ask you what your name and address is.
    . . . .

Police officer: Do you agree that on the [date given] you were spoken to by myself here at this Police station?
Interviewee: Yes, that's right.
Police officer: And on that day, using an interpreter, a statement was taken from you in relation to what you knew in relation to the death of Mr. A?
Interviewee: That's right, yes.
Police officer: Do you agree that when this statement was taken you signed an acknowledgement in which you said 'I hereby acknowledge that this statement is true and correct and I make it in the belief that a person making a false statement in the circumstances is liable to the penalties of perjury', and did you sign that statement?
Interviewee: That's right.
Police officer: In that statement you said . . .

This is a verbatim police record. Note that the police officer alternates between first and third person usage in relation to the interviewee, and also that this otherwise relatively straightforward interview involves the reading out of a formal *written* passage of text on the part of the officer. The reading out of such passages typically forms part of re-interviews.

Lawyer/client conferences

These may take place in a solicitor's office, in a barrister's chambers or, where bail has been refused, in police custody or in gaol. They tend to follow the same pattern as for other diagnostic interviews, with the lawyers asking most of the questions designed to elicit information and to ascertain facts prior to presenting possible solutions to the problem.

Interpreting at a lawyer/client conference tends to be less stressful than at police interviews or in court, but equally important and difficult, as at this stage important legal advice is given and major strategic decisions made by the client.

This excerpt from a transcript of a lawyer/client conference through an interpreter illustrates the kind of language that some lawyers use in their interviews:

Lawyer/client conference

> Lawyer: Right, he has been charged by the police alleging that on the 17th May this year at Springvale he did drive carelessly on a highway to wit Heatherton Road, does he firstly know what careless driving is?
> Client: Yes, I know.
> Lawyer: Right, he holds a licence I take it.
> Client: Yes.
> Lawyer: Right, how long has he held a licence in the state of Victoria?
> Client: About eight years.
> Lawyer: Eight years. Can he describe to me what happened on the day this offence occurred or was alleged to have occurred?
> (Campbell and D'Argaville, 1992: 108)

Most lawyers, prosecution and defence lawyers alike, when interviewing an accused or a witness who will have to give evidence in court, will try to take the client through the process of giving evidence-in-chief (i.e. giving evidence by way of answering questions from one's own lawyer). Sometimes a lawyer will closely question the client, testing and challenging the testimony. By such cross-examination prior to the actual hearing, the lawyer will be able firstly to assess the client's ability to stand up to real cross-examination in court and, secondly, to give the client a taste of what to expect.

Likewise the lawyer/client conference will provide valuable practice for the interpreter, who will also learn a great deal about the facts of the case during the interview. It is important for interpreters to bear in mind that information learned during such interviews must not interfere with interpreting in court for the same case.

At a committal hearing in 1988 in Victoria, Australia, the victim of an armed robbery took the witness stand and was asked through an interpreter whether she was able to identify the offender. The reply in the other language was 'No', but the interpreter then said to the witness in that language: 'You can't say that. Before this you told the Police that you could. You can't change it now.' Considerable verbal exchange took place along this line, while the barristers and the magistrate demanded to know what was going on. Finally, the witness said 'Alright then, yes', and the interpreter said 'Yes'.

This is an extremely rare, extraordinary and unforgivable action by an unethical 'interpreter' who in all probability was untrained and unaccredited. But it demonstrates what can happen if an interpreter allows prior knowledge of the facts of the case and an inadequate understanding of legal propriety to interfere with the interpreting task. The importance of preparing oneself for an interpreting assignment has been stressed elsewhere in this book, but it is important to emphasize here that the information gained during briefing, whilst useful in preparing specialist terminology and understanding the context of the case, must not interfere with the interpreting performance, especially in court.

Court work

This includes *interpreting for clients* giving evidence-in-chief, being cross-examined and re-examined, and *interpreting for the accused* to enable him or her to follow all exchanges in the court and thus be 'linguistically present' in the proceedings (*Gradidge v. Grace Brothers Pty Ltd* (1988) 93 FLR [Federal Law Reports] 414).

The interpreter works in a very tense, public atmosphere and very often for parties with hostile intentions. The great majority of cases are dealt with in the lower courts, which are often crowded and noisy. The pace is fast and sometimes a case is over before the person concerned realizes it; the distance between interlocutors is great; and the acoustics are often poor. This combination means that the court environment itself is a hindrance to effective interpreting. The higher courts are much more sedate and formal. To a person unfamiliar with the legal system, the proceedings can be quite overwhelming. The language used is legalistic, but arguably needs to be so to convey all technical aspects of the law. The concepts and principles underlying legal reasoning are strongly culturally bound and the rules governing the conduct of the participants are largely procedural.

The following three extracts from court records illustrate the kind of content, both in terms of subject matter and language used, that an interpreter can expect in a court assignment. They all concern the same prosecution witness. The first extract is from evidence-in-chief, the second is from cross-examination and the third is from re-examination.

Evidence-in-chief of a prosecution witness

> Prosecutor: Could you tell the members of the jury what happened on the next occasion?
> Witness: The next occasion was [date given], Tuesday. If I remember correctly, it was Tuesday about lunchtime, 12.00, 12.30.
> Prosecutor: What happened?
> Witness: I was working in my shop ... The accused entered with another gentleman. He strolled right up to where I was. The accomplice stood at the entrance to the shop. The accused came up to me, said he wanted to talk to me, it was urgent. He grabbed me and made a demand on me for $10,000.
> Prosecutor: What did you do?
> Witness: I tried to talk to him ...
> Prosecutor: What happened next?
> Witness: He motioned beside me and pulled out a gun which he up into me side, into me stomach.
> Prosecutor: Would you look at this item; are you able to identify that?
> Witness: Yes, I can remember that.
> Prosecutor: What is it?
> Witness: I don't know about guns, but some sort of gun I presume.
> Prosecutor: Perhaps if I could have that marked for identification at this stage, Your Honour.
> Judge: Exhibit C ... Pistol for identification.

Cross-examination of the witness

> Defence barrister: My client had this gun to your head whilst you were doing that?
> Witness: No, he had it pointed into my stomach.
> Defence barrister: Did you see the gun; did he show you the gun?
> Witness: Yes.
> Defence barrister: He showed you?

Witness: Yes.
Defence barrister: Could I just have Exhibit C please? (To witness): He showed you that, did he—it is a cap gun, is it not?
Witness: I don't know, is it—I've never seen it?
Defence barrister: Have a look—what did you just say?
Witness: I've never seen it up close—I've seen it, but I've never seen it.
Defence barrister: Never seen it, or never seen it up close, which one is it?
Witness: Well, I've seen it—how can I tell a cap gun if you just show me a gun?
Defence barrister: Why did you say to the ladies and gentlemen of the jury, 'I've never seen it'?
Witness: You asked a question—
Defence barrister: Answer my question please, witness.
Witness: I've seen it.
Defence barrister: Look, we all heard you say a minute ago, 'I've never seen it'—now, why did you say that?
Witness: I had seen it because he showed it to me.
Defence barrister: You answer my question please, and I will ask it all afternoon until you do—why did you say to the ladies and gentlemen of the jury, 'I've never seen it'?
Judge: Are you able to answer the question?
Witness: Well, I have seen it.
Judge: That is not an answer to the question you were asked.
Witness: Yes.
Judge: You may or may not be able to answer the question, but the question was, why did you say, in this court, a short time ago, that you had never seen the gun?
Witness: Cause he's referring to the pop when he pulled it out and showed it. I–I was referring to—what he was asking me then.
Defence barrister: Indeed, and I will ask the question again—why did you say, 'I've never seen it'?
Witness: I can't answer you that.
Defence barrister: Why not? (No reply)
Defence barrister: Why not, witness? (No reply)
Defence barrister: Why not, witness?
Witness: Because I don't know why I just said it—I just said—

> Defence barrister: The answer, and I suggest the reason why, is that at no stage did you see such a thing, because at no stage did he ever brandish or use, or even mention such a thing?
>
> Witness: Yes, he did.
>
> Defence barrister: I put it to you in fact that you simply were not robbed at all on the [date given]?
>
> Witness: I was.

The tone and language can then change quite abruptly when a witness is re-examined by their own side, as illustrated by this extract from a re-examination of the same witness to clarify matters arising out of a cross-examination:

Re-examination of the witness

> Prosecutor: Mr. A., my learned friend asked you about an occasion—you said there was an occasion which he offered you money, do you recall saying that?
>
> Witness: He offered me money?
>
> Prosecutor: He offered money—expressed to be repayment of the money and drugs, is that right?
>
> Witness: He never offered me money—he mentioned of—'I'll pay you back'.
>
> Prosecutor: All right, what was your understanding of that statement?
>
> Witness: Well, my understanding of that statement was that that money that was given to him, right, on the occasion where he demanded money from me, that he was going to pay me back, but I didn't know whether that'd be the case or not.

Another task for the interpreter is to keep the accused 'linguistically present' during presentation of various arguments by counsel. The following is an extract from a legal submission made by a defence barrister. After successfully arguing for a number of charges or 'counts' to be dropped, the defence barrister sums up his submission as follows:

Legal submission by a defence barrister

> Defence barrister: That leaves Your Honour, in my respectful submission, only three counts on the presentment, 15, 16 and 18,

which it is submitted, there is evidence of. Those three counts all, in my submission, must fall in the absence of an acceptance of Miss. A's evidence. There is nothing else beyond her evidence, in my respectful submission, those three counts could well, given all that Your Honour knows about the case, be the subject of an invitation by Your Honour under the Prasad rule, which is not, of course, within the meaning of Doney. Doney is external to that.

Judge: Yes.

Defence barrister: Doney is concerned with where there is evidence which can go to the jury, as good and as succinct a definition can be found in Cross. I'm referring to the penultimate edition, the Third Edition of Cross, on page 293 where the learned authors say this: 'The third procedure is the Proussard invitation'.

Judge: No, I think there is a distinction. No, continue anyway.

Defence barrister: Yes, Your Honour. The Proussard invitation is not a commonly used thing, certainly. But it is an invitation in an appropriate case for the jury to say they don't want to hear anymore. It is not an unsafe submission of course, because that is prohibited by Attorney-General No. 1 and Queen and Doney. It is not a submission of no case to answer, because there is some evidence. It is really a matter for Your Honour, on the remaining counts, to extend such an invitation.

Note that the language is highly condensed, makes continual reference to other cases and authorities, and assumes contextual knowledge of the legal system. As such its interpretation in the other language is just as intimidating and confusing, if not more so, to the non-English speaking client. A number of critics therefore have argued that the legal system needs reforms that would address broader issues over and above the provision of interpreters (Laster and Taylor, 1994).

At the end of a case, if the accused is found guilty, the defence lawyer will put further pleas to the judge regarding sentencing. After listening to all matters relevant to sentencing, the judge will determine the sentence, as in this extract from a sentencing by a judge after a plea for mitigation:

Sentencing by a judge

> Judge: Well, occasionally I go out on a limb and I suppose this is one of them, but we will see what happens. Mr A, stop me if you do not understand what I am saying.
>
> Prisoner: Yes.
>
> Judge: You have pleaded guilty to one count of armed robbery. It is a very serious crime indeed and it is also a crime which is frequently committed in our community. The maximum sentence imposed by Parliament as adjusted is now 20 years in gaol. Do you understand that?
>
> Prisoner: Yes.
>
> . . . . . .
>
> Judge: ... General deterrence is probably the most relevant of all sentencing considerations so far as this crime of armed robbery is concerned, and really this case is no exception to the general rule. Deterrence to you as an individual is also important and I bear in mind that I should impose a sentence which will deter you from committing this type of crime in the future and which may deter other young men and women ... I have taken account of the matters set out in the pre-sentence report ... I have also taken account of your plea of guilty, an early plea of guilty ... If you break the terms of the community based order that I'm prepared to grant you, then it is highly likely that you will be placed in a youth training centre to serve a period of detention. It may be that you could even end up in jail, so just bear that in mind. Do you understand?
>
> Prisoner: Yes.
>
> [In this jurisdiction, a community-based order is a non-custodial alternative to prison.]

THE INTERPRETER'S ROLE

In Chapter 3, it is argued that there are two dimensions to the role of interpreters: the interpreting function itself and the context in which the interpreting function is performed. In legal settings there is inherent conflict between the role of interpreters as facilitators of communication and the role assigned to interpreters by the legal system. The potential dangers arising from this conflict need to be recognized.

As facilitators of communication

The aim of legal interpreting is to facilitate meaningful participation by non-speakers of English in the legal process (D'Argaville, 1991; Laster and Taylor, 1994), i.e. to aid in the communication process. Interpreting is not about changing one set of labels into another set of labels in another language. Rather, it involves decoding a spoken message transmitted in a particular context, and then encoding and delivering that message in another language so that it has the same meaning for and impact upon the listener as it would for a listener of the same language.

The *decoding process* includes:

- distilling the meaning from the form used by the speaker—a relation which rarely, if ever, matches at word level;
- understanding the logical relationship between what is being said and the rest of the text, i.e. grasping the essential semantic structure of the speech as it is being delivered;
- recognizing the various stylistic devices employed by the speaker. For example, in answering the question 'How often do you see your brother?' the response 'I see my brother once in a blue moon' is not about the moon's colour. However, in a psychiatric forensic interview, the exchange, 'Describe the moon', 'The moon is round and pink', does address colour and must be interpreted literally.

Thus the interpreter's licence clearly transcends word-level considerations. In fact, global and non-lingual considerations are generally far more important. But interpreters are *not* free to add or to omit any elements (Gentile, 1991; Berk-Seligson, 1990). Indeed the interpreter's licence is firmly bound by the concept of *accuracy*:

> The transfer of message must be complete, the interpreter can not take upon himself or herself to summarise what the client says nor to omit any element contained in the message, no matter how relevant or

otherwise the interpreter feels that element to be to the situation. Accuracy also means that the impact of the message must be maintained. (Gentile, 1991: 30–1)

In the context of legal interpreting, the importance of accuracy cannot be overemphasized, as any inconsistency in a witness's account can damage the credibility of that witness. The earlier extract from cross-examination of a witness shows how, in the hands of a skilful barrister, such an inconsistency can be brought out in a dramatic manner. The following case underlines both the importance of accuracy and the difficulties that interpreters face. The accused was charged with molesting his daughter. His wife was called to give evidence and was asked in English, 'is your husband infatuated with your daughter?'. Apparently the interpreter found this extremely difficult to interpret into the other language and rendered it as 'Does your husband love your daughter?'. The wife answered in the affirmative. (Commonwealth Attorney-General's Department, 1991: 48)

The role assigned by the legal system

The notion that interpreting 'word for word', 'sentence for sentence' or 'literally' is accurate interpreting betrays a high degree of naivety and ignorance of the process of interpreting. Yet for reasons directly related to legal principles, the courts have given judgments that define the role of interpreters very narrowly.

The legal *raison d'être* of court interpreters is derived from the common law right to a fair trial, a component of which is the right of an accused to be present at his trial. Mere physical presence is not enough, as stated by Lord Reading in *R. v. Lee Kun* (1916 1KB337): 'The presence of the accused means not only that he must physically be in attendance, but also that he must be capable of understanding the nature of the proceedings'. This line of reasoning is reflected in the arguments of the 'right to he heard' or the right to be 'linguistically present' (Bird, 1991; Berk-Seligson, 1990).

Thus, while it is clear that the legal system regards the role of interpreters as primarily that of communication, it is also committed to legal principles which have led to judgments on the role of legal interpreters. We are interested in two aspects of the way the legal system perceives the role of interpreters: how and what interpreters are expected to interpret.

How to interpret

Being a late entrant and a relatively powerless participant in the legal system, interpreters have had to conform to established legal principles. One such principle is *the rule against hearsay*, expressed simply as 'hearsay is not evidence'. The relevance of this legal principle to interpreting lies in the fact that when a prosecutor presents a record of interview taken through an interpreter as evidence of the accused, it might be argued that, as essentially it is what the interpreter repeated from what she or he heard from the accused, it is hearsay and therefore not admissible as evidence.

This point was raised in *Gaio v. R.* (1960) [Australian] 104 CLR [Commonwealth Law Reports] 419. The High Court of Australia held that the record of an interview given through an interpreter was admissible as evidence of the accused. Among other legal argument, the judges observed that the interpreter is essentially a 'translating machine', a bilingual transmitter 'not different in principle from that which in another case an electrical instrument might fulfil in overcoming the barrier of distance' (Kitto J. at 430).

Most people have interpreted this judgement as meaning that the legal system assigns interpreters a very narrow linguistic licence, and thus it has attracted a great deal of criticism (Laster, 1990). Some argue that Gaio was a ruling on admissibility of evidence and should not be taken to be a statement from the court on the nature of interpreting (Roberts-Smith, 1990; Commonwealth Attorney-General's Department, 1991). However, some judges still expect interpreters to provide 'literal interpreting' and most still hold that 'the conduit or machine model is still the official legal position and, by implication, the way they [interpreters] should be used' (D'Argaville, 1991: 40).

In the context of this chapter, Gaio is instructive not for the rights or wrongs of the argument but because it shows the extent to which legal principles can profoundly influence the work of interpreters in a legal setting.

What to interpret

American jurists have argued successfully, with constitutional support, for the right to be 'linguistically present' in court, leading to legislation such as the Federal Court Interpreters Act 1978 which defines the circumstances where court interpreters will be provided to enable the accused to understand what happens in court (US Congress, Senate, Committee on the Judiciary, Sub-committee on the Constitution 1986). Implicit is the view already expressed in *R. v. Lee Kun* that mere physical presence is insufficient and that the accused must understand the proceedings. The major implication is that interpreters do not just interpret for the witnesses when they take the witness stand, but also interpret for the accused all other exchanges that take place in court.

This view was expressed in a similar fashion in the judgment by Mr Justice Samuels in the New South Wales Court of Appeals (*Gradidge v. Grace Brothers Pty Ltd* (1988) [Australian] 93 FLR [Federal Law Reports] 414):

> It must be that any party who is unable to (for want of some physical capacity or for lack of knowledge of the language of the court) understand what is happening must, by the use of an interpreter, be placed in the position in which he or she should be in if those defects did not exist. The task of the interpreter in short is to remove any barriers which prevent understanding or communication ... The task of the interpreter is not restricted merely to passing on the questions when the party is giving evidence; it must be extended also to appraising a party of what is happening in the court and of what procedures are being conducted at a particular time. (Commonwealth Attorney-General's Department, 1991: 43)

The implication for interpreters is clear. When the non-English speaking client takes the witness stand, the interpreter is expected to provide interpreting for evidence-in-chief, cross-examination and re-examination. When other witnesses give evidence in English and when judges and lawyers speak, the interpreter is expected to interpret, simultaneously as practicality would dictate, all matters into the language of the client. This represents the legal system's expectation of what interpreters should interpret.

One interesting observation is that whereas in earlier cases, like Gaio, the judiciary was concerned with legal points (admissibility of evidence given through interpreters), the later case, Gradidge, reflects an awakening on the part of the judiciary to the broader role of interpreters in relation to the effects on the person concerned.

Summary of role

The perception of the role of interpreters in legal settings is far from uniform. Most agree that interpreters are 'language experts', but confusion still reigns as to what this means. While interpreters take the view that the interpreting task is a holistic, multi-faceted and meaning-based process, other participants take the narrow 'conduit pipe' view, which stands squarely against the accepted role of interpreters as facilitators of communication.

Legal interpreters serve two masters: the communication needs of the parties concerned and the formal requirements of the legal system. While the latter is clearly very important, the communication needs of the parties demand that the broader view of the role of interpreters must prevail.

TYPES OF DISCOURSE

As in mental health interpreting, legal interpreters face different types of discourse ranging from narrative everyday language to highly fragmented discourse. In an adversarial legal system, legal settings fall into two broad categories:

- *those occasions where the interlocutors have a genuine need to communicate* for the purpose of obtaining information (lawyer/client conferences), persuading the other party (legal submission), explaining (judge's instructions) etc.;
- *those events which are not exercises in communication but dramas played out for another party*–the judge and/or jury (evidence-in-chief, cross-examinations and re-examinations).

This distinction is very helpful in that it explains many important features of legal discourse.

Interpreting in legal settings where information is sought, such as police interviews or lawyer interviews, does not differ in any major way to interpreting in other domains. There are variations in terms of atmosphere, terminology used, power relationships, strategic importance to the case, consequences for the parties involved, but in essence these interviews tend to follow similar patterns to those discussed earlier in this book.

Note, however, that some friendly police interviews can turn into hostile interviews. This happens when the police initially regard the interviewee as a witness but then, due to information received during the interview, have reasons to treat the interviewee as a suspect. Some jurisdictions require the police, at the point that they begin to form such suspicion, to provide a verbal 'caution' informing the interviewee of the right to remain silent and that anything said may be taken as evidence in a court of law. The lack of such 'caution' may render the record of interview inadmissible at a later court hearing.

As most aspects of interpreting in interviews have been dealt with elsewhere in this book, our attention now focuses on the second category of evidence. Evidence-in-chief, cross-examination and re-examination constitute a major part of court-room discourse, the features of which are demonstrated by this extract from the cross-examination of a witness:

Cross-examination

> Lawyer: I understand you to say you saw the testator sign this document?
> Witness: I did.
> Lawyer: And did you sign, at his request, as subscribing witness?
> Witness: I did.
> Lawyer: Was it sealed with red or black wax?
> Witness: With red wax.
> Lawyer: Did you see him seal it with red wax?
> Witness: I did.
> Lawyer: Where was the testator when he signed and sealed this will?
> Witness: In his bed.

Lawyer: Pray, how long a piece of red wax did he use?
Witness: About three inches long.
Lawyer: And who gave the testator this piece of red wax?
Witness: I did.
Lawyer: Where did you get it?
Witness: From the drawer of his desk.
Lawyer: How did he melt that piece of wax?
Witness: With a candle.
Lawyer: Where did the candle come from?
Witness: I got it out of the cupboard in the room.
Lawyer: How long should you say the candle was?
Witness: Perhaps four or five inches long.
Lawyer: Do you remember who lit the candle?
Witness: I lit it.
Lawyer: What did you light it with?
Witness: Why, with a match.
Lawyer: Where did you get the match?
Witness: On the mantel-shelf in the room.
Lawyer: Now, sir, upon your solemn oath, you saw the testator sign this will—he signed it in his bed—at his request you signed it as a subscribing witness— you saw him seal it—a piece of wax about three inches long—he lit the wax with a piece of candle which you procured from a cupboard—you lit the candle with a match you found on a mantel-shelf?
Witness: I did.
Lawyer: Once more, sir—upon your solemn oath you did?
Witness: I did.
Lawyer: My lord, you will observe that this will is sealed with a wafer! (Munkman, 1951: 85–6)

What characterises this cross-examination is the fact that the cross-examiner has no desire to communicate with the witness to ascertain the facts of the case. The only intention is to demonstrate to the jury that the witness is a complete and hopeless liar.

Interpreters must be aware of the different implications of the combative cross-examination and the non-combative giving of evidence-in-chief.

Evidence-in-chief

When a witness gives evidence-in-chief, a rehearsed drama is played out by two participants sharing the common goal of relating a mutually understood story to an audience. In this co-operative effort, the lawyer is clear, patient and mostly chronological in approach, and uses open questions to allow the witness every opportunity to tell his or her story. Nevertheless, even in this non-combative courtroom drama, the discourse style is different from everyday language because the giving of evidence in court is bound by a set of rules of evidence. Conley and O'Barr have noted that these rules of evidence operate to remove the following features of everyday language from court-room discourse: reported speech, which the court treats as hearsay; expressions of opinions, conclusions and generalizations, which can be deemed as incompetent or irrelevant. (Conley and O'Barr, 1990: 16–17)

The following extracts illustrate how these features of everyday language are excluded from courtroom discourse:

Reported speech regarded as hearsay

> Lawyer: Now could you describe the year or approximate year?
> Witness: Uh, seventy—I was told seventy-three.
> Lawyer: Object, your honour, to what she was told.
> Judge: Sustained as to what she was told. Disabuse your mind of that, members of the jury. It is not competent.
> Lawyer: Could you describe whether it looked like a new or an old car?
> Witness: Well, it was seventy-three then. It was a seventy-three Pontiac. (Conley and O'Barr, 1990: 16)

Generalization disallowed

> Lawyer: After you entered the fifty-five zone, what happened next?
> Witness: Um, our cars have the electronic siren and I tapped it a few times hoping he would pull over because, uh, sometimes when people try to run they wait till they get to open road and so I was trying to get him to stop—

Lawyer: Objection. Motion to strike.
Judge: Sustained as to what people sometimes do. Disabuse your mind of that, members of the jury. It is not competent. Motion to strike is allowed. (Conley and O'Barr, 1990: 18)

In cases where a witness gives evidence through an interpreter, the objection will be voiced only after the witness has completed an utterance and the interpreter has interpreted at least a part of it into English. The barrister is thus interrupting the interpreter, not the witness—the originator of the utterance. This raises interesting theoretical considerations, as the original utterance in the other language is a closed text which cannot be interrupted. From a theoretical perspective, the interpreter has no choice but to complete its interpretation into English. From a practical angle, however, interpreters often halt the interpretation to wait for the judge to announce whether the objection is sustained or overruled. If the objection is overruled, having put the rest of the witness statement on mental hold, the interpreter will continue with it and then explain to the witness what has just happened. If the objection is sustained, the interpreter will explain to the witness that the judge ruled in favour of the objection by the opposing barrister.

More often, it is the questions of the barrister that are objected to, as in the following extract from the transcript of a United States case involving a Spanish–English interpreter:

Objection to a question by the opposing barrister

Defense attorney [barrister]: And she has been living in San Diego for about six years?
Interpreter: Y ella ha estado viviendo en San Diego como seis anos?
Prosecuting attorney: I object your honor.
Interpreter [addressing the witness]: Momentito, objeto la licenciada Ellsworth. (Just a moment, Miss Ellsworth has objected.)
Judge: The objection's overruled.
Interpreter: Overruled, sir?
Judge: Yes.
Interpreter [addressing the attorney]: Uh, the defendant answered 'yes', sir.

[Because of the overlapping of the attorney's and the interpreter's speech, the witness's barely audible affirmative response, 'Sí', is lost amidst the loud objection and the concurrent Spanish interpreting.]
(Berk-Seligson, 1990: 83-4)

In summary, a witness giving evidence-in-chief is not 'communication' in the everyday sense of the word. It is a kind of rehearsed drama played for the benefit of an audience—the jury—punctuated by occasional objection from the opposing barrister in accordance with the court's rules governing the giving of evidence.

Cross-examination

In contrast, cross-examination is an unrehearsed performance characterized by a strong element of combat. The barrister, in a non-linear approach (the hop, skip, jump technique) seeks to deny the witness full expression. The aims of cross-examination are to destroy or to weaken the evidence-in-chief, to elicit new evidence helpful to the party cross-examining and to undermine the witness. Turn-taking opportunities assume greater importance as the barrister attempts to discredit the witness and the witness tries to persuade the jury as the following transcript shows:

Cross-examination

>A[nswer]: Yes, because he was drunk and—
>Q[uestion]: Well, how do you know that he was drunk? When was the last time you'd seen him?
>A: Because my, my father goes to bed when he's not. He doesn't—he's a different person. There's two differ—
>Q: When was the last time before this incident that you had seen your father?
>A: Oh, probably the day before.
>Q: And you, uh, you did not see him the day before until the police officer down and opened the door, and you give this court the opinion that he was drunk, is that correct?
>A: Well he is my father and I know him quite well.

Q: You, you just assume that he was drunk, is that correct?
A: No, I'm not assuming, no.
Q: Well, what now, what do you base your testimony on that he was drunk?
A: Well, I know him, that's the difference. When you've lived with a person, when you've grown up with him all your life, you know him.
Q: And you know he's always drunk, is that correct?
A: I know when he is and when he isn't.
Q: Wha–, even though you don't see him or don't talk to him?
A: That's right, that's right (O'Barr, 1982: 168)

[Note that the cross-examiner twice interrupted the witness's answer.]

With our focus still on the discourse style characteristic of evidence-in-chief, cross-examination and re-examination, we will now examine the impact of interpreter performance on a court case.

IMPACT ON A COURT CASE

The quality of decision-making at each stage from the investigation process to the trial obviously depends on the quality of information available to the decision-makers. The prosecutor's decision on whether or not a suspect is charged must be based on evidence available, an important part of which is the police record of interview. The quality of advice given by solicitor to client, and the soundness of decisions made by the client—say, whether or not to plead guilty—depend on the quality of information available at the lawyer/client conference. The strategy and effectiveness of the barrister's conduct of a case and, perhaps even more importantly, the final decision by a judge, a magistrate or a jury, depend on how they perceive all relevant facts as the case unfolds.

Given that at every stage the participants rely on interpreters to overcome the language barriers, then the quality of decisions, advice, strategy and judgement must depend in part on the quality of the interpreted information. Clearly there exists a nexus between the outcome of a case and the work of the interpreters involved—though interpretation is only one of the many complex factors in any case.

The impact of interpreters on trial by jury has been noted by Berk-Seligson (1990). Studying the performance of Spanish–English court interpreters in the United States, she found that interpreters do intrude into the communication dynamics of the court-room, alter speech styles, add or omit elements such as qualifiers, hedgings, terms of politeness etc. Furthermore, by studying the impact on mock juries, she found that the presence of polite markers had an impact on how the jurors view the witness.

We will now focus on the impact of interpreters on the communication dynamics of a court-room cross-examination in terms of turn-taking opportunities by the participants.

Turn-taking opportunities in cross-examination

In a non-combative interview, both participants follow well established conventions to determine who has the 'turn' at each juncture of the discourse. There are also well established ways of indicating whether a speaker wishes to retain that turn or to pass it to another person.

The communication dynamics of a cross-examination are different. The participants often, if not always, have conflicting aims, and compete to be heard. Turn-taking opportunities available to or denied each participant are thus of great importance. What happens, some say too often, is that when a segment to be interpreted gets too long, the interpreter, mostly by body language, signs or vocalized language, interrupts and begins interpreting. In a non-combative interview this may not be a problem, as both participants are working towards communicating with one another. In a cross-examination, however, these break-points present opportunities for the other participant to take the floor and deny the opponent's turn.

At a crucial stage in a case, taking the turn from your opponent can have devastating effects, as the following example shows. This example, while hypothetical, stems from a case observed by the author in which an earlier witness, Mr A, had given evidence that seemed to be damaging to the accused. When the accused took the witness box, the prosecutor, understandably, wanted to put him on the spot. The following exchange took place:

8 Legal Settings

Cross-examination: Exchange A

Barrister: You have heard what Mr A said in his statement to the Police. What do you say to that?

Interpreter: Anh có nghe những lời ông A khai với cảnh sát đó. Vậy thì anh nói như thế nào đây?

Accused: Nó nói như vậy thì cũng dễ hiểu thôi. Nếu như tôi là nó thì tôi cũng nói như vậy.[*] Bởi vì là trong vụ này chỉ có hai đứa có thể bị nghi là thủ phạm, là tôi với nó. Thành ra khi nó khai với cảnh sát thì đương nhiên nó phải khai như vậy cho cảnh sát khỏi nghi ngờ nó.

Interpreter: That's quite understandable. I would have said the same thing if I was in his shoes.[*] The reason being that there are only two people who could be suspected of having committed this offence, he and I. Therefore when he made the statement with the Police, it's quite natural that he made such a statement in order that the Police would not suspect him.

Barrister: Mr A and you were good friends, is that correct?

Interpreter: Ông A và anh trước đây là bạn thân, phải không?

Accused: Vâng.

Interpreter: Yes

[*] Had the interpreter decided to interpret at this point in the reply, the exchange might have taken a very different turn, to become something like this:

Cross-examination: Exchange B

Barrister: You have heard what Mr A said in his statement to the Police. What do you say to that?

Interpreter: Anh có nghe những lời ông A khai với cảnh sát đó. Vậy thì anh nói như thế nào đây?

Accused: Nó nói như vậy thì cũng dễ hiểu thôi. Nếu như tôi là nó thì tôi cũng nói như vậy.[*]

Interpreter: That's quite understandable. I would have said the same thing if I was in his shoes.

Barrister: Good. Mr A and you were good friends, is that correct?

Interpreter: Ông A và anh trước đây là bạn thân, phải không?

113

Accused: Vâng.
Interpreter: Yes

[*] Clearly, when the interpreter decided to start interpreting at this point and the barrister decided to continue the questioning, the accused was denied his turn and hence his opportunity to complete what he wanted to say, with the potential of leaving the jury with the impression that the accused broadly agreed with what witness A had said.

Thus, when interpreting for a client being cross-examined, an additional dimension must be considered: the interpreter must not deprive the client of their turn-taking opportunities. The general rule applies that when a segment becomes too long it is better to begin interpreting than to risk misinterpreting. But the interpreter must bear in mind that interrupting a person effectively takes their turn away, and it is the responsibility of the interpreter to give it back. Practical strategies to achieve this include using a rising intonation at the end of a segment to indicate that there is more to come, or maintaining eye contact to encourage the client to continue. Remember that appropriate strategies may well be language or culture specific.

Considerations based on turn-taking opportunities, a unique feature of liaison interpreting, are important in all settings, but in cross-examination they assume much greater importance and require special attention.

In summary, legal interpreting is an area that holds many fears for interpreters, particularly interpreters new to the profession or with no legal background. One peculiarity of legal interpreting, particularly in court, is that the role of the interpreter has from time to time been defined as an instrument of the legal process:

- as a 'conduit' of discourse;
- as having particular responsibilities, (e.g. to ensure that a party is 'linguistically present').

It is crucial to remember that these definitions are not necessarily based upon views of language or communication, but upon the particular imperatives of the legal system, and jurisprudential or even constitutional requirements.

Particularly in court settings, the interpreter must deal with very different types of discourse, some of which will depart radically from intuitive assumptions of language-as-communication. For example, cross-examination is essentially a play of language for the benefit of jury or judge, and departs crucially from standard dialogue interpreting. Interpreters must be comfortable in situations where one party is explicitly *not* responding to what the other party wants to communicate.

9 Business Settings

What do we mean by interpreting in business settings? In the narrowest sense, the term denotes two or more business people discussing business matters through an interpreter. Stereotypical examples include importer/exporter negotiations; discussions between the local head of a subsidiary company and the foreign owner of the company; and discussions between a local business person and an overseas consultant, perhaps on taxation, investment, industrial relations, import tariffs etc. However, we take interpreting in business settings in its broadest possible sense, to include all interpreting situations which are outside the welfare/medical/legal rubric. We do not include relationships characterized by a marked differential in power or status within a given society. Examples of these interpreting settings range from arts, sport, tourism and recreation to patent negotiations or government-to-government meetings and delegations.

This categorization is not absolute and practitioners in different parts of the world may call this setting commercial, trade or diplomatic. The demands made upon interpreters require particular skills and techniques.

The physical environment

Interpreting in business settings is not confined to office environments. It may take place in a variety of environments from the factory floor to an aircraft, from a plant room to a restaurant. This variety often requires adjustment to the mode of interpreting. For example, on the factory floor, the interpreter accompanying a visiting party may need to use *chuchotage*—because the noise level, the number of participants and the acoustic characteristics of the environment are such that only two or three people can hear what the interpreter is saying. This in turn will encourage other members of the party to seek from the interpreter, at a later time, the information they have missed.

The conclusion of successful business negotiations may include a public presentation of the results, with the interpreter called upon to perform consecutive interpreting for a large group.

When an interpreter is travelling abroad with a delegation, the change in physical environment produces changes in mood, attitude and reactions of the members of the delegation. The interpreter should be aware that these will affect the communication style of the delegation. Furthermore, if the interpreter is the only link with the host culture, being the only one to speak that language, he/she may need to assume additional roles including that of a public relations officer and secretary, and to take care of such tasks as collecting documents, writing minutes, booking hotels and paying bills. The interpreter is more likely to be called upon to play a more generalized 'cultural bridge' role when the differences between the cultures are vast. The delegation will rely on the interpreter to avoid embarrassment and to smooth the way should any problem occur.

It is thus clear that the interpreter may be required regularly to switch from one task to another, even from one role to another. The multiplicity of roles can make inordinate demands on the interpreter's time and concentration—being 'on duty' perhaps from breakfast to late evening, and having to deal with sometimes competing demands from members of the delegation. While ideally many of these roles would be performed by hired agents or other bilingual delegate members, this may not have been arranged, leaving the interpreter to deal with management as well as interpreting.

The nature of the subject matter

In business settings, the interpreting function, in relation to the subject matter, approximates that in conference contexts. The discussions are often specific and detailed and cover such things as commercial arrangements, production and warehousing techniques, contracts and deadlines, specific descriptions of products or detailed arrangements for delivery and payments.

Interpreters will find very different levels of readiness on the part of companies or agencies to adequately brief them. Depending on the nature of negotiation or meeting, some will provide detailed information on the company's products, services, structure, objectives, and what specifically is to be talked about. In other cases, efforts by the interpreter to obtain specific documentation prior to the meeting/discussion may receive very little response because of the confidential nature and commercial sensitivity of the information. This means that the interpreter is often left to prepare for such assignments to a level of generality of information which is only mildly useful for the meeting.

For instance, the interpreter might simply be briefed that the discussion will be about the production of plastic tubing. The interpreter can only anticipate to some extent the direction of the discussions and prepare by becoming familiar with current methods of production of plastic tubing. However, the discussion may include new production methods developed by the companies, it may concern itself with a single step in the production process, or it may concentrate on the manipulation of materials to facilitate a certain production method. In short, for the interpreter, the level of unpredictability of the direction of the discussion is high. This has implications for the techniques employed.

The interpreting team

The host country or firm often provides interpreter(s) to work for both parties. Even when each party provides its own interpreter (in-house or freelance), it is common for the interpreters to work out between themselves who will interpret in which direction. Exceptions occur when one party (in particular, a senior politician) insists that his/her own interpreter work in a particular direction. Commonly, each interpreter works into his/her second language, the reasons being that the interpreter is familiar with the client's accent, cultural background and topical context. This is different from conference interpreting where the interpreter usually works into his/her first language. Alternatively, interpreters may decide to divide the work on the basis of time, with each working in both directions for a given time.

For interpreters who have previously worked together, the likelihood of problems arising is minimal; they will be familiar with each other's performance and can enhance the total service provision by drawing on each other's strengths. When there is no shared experience, there must be a discussion before the interpreting begins.

It is particularly important to counter the client's perception, often expectation, that their interpreter is an instrument of quality control of the other interpreter's performance. Such perceptions may be in conflict with the professional obligations of the interpreter. This becomes a real issue if one of the interpreters commits an error. The other interpreter must make a judgement on the seriousness of the error and, if necessary, notify his/her colleague, who in turn must deal with it. It is important to stress that it does not serve any purpose to comment on a colleague's minor lapses. The ethical issues arising from this and similar situations will be dealt with below.

Some observations on negotiation

Negotiation is the process of reaching agreement between parties who begin from different bargaining positions. Many business meetings consist mainly of negotiations. While any interaction can include negotiation as a technique for achieving objectives, it can be argued that business interactions are distinguished by the fact that negotiation is their central objective.

Knowledge of the negotiating styles adopted by different cultural groups is of paramount importance for successful interpreting. The interpreter must be familiar with these styles, which largely emerge through a combination of behaviours and only some of which are linguistic. They include the degree of directness, the willingness or ability to reach a decision or make that decision known during the meeting, the capacity to deviate from previous correspondence, the means used to express degrees of agreement or disagreement to propositions, the role of ceremony and protocol in the negotiation, the expectations as to the sequencing of elements in the negotiation, the expectations relating to dress, food and body language.

During the course of a meeting, the parties may need to discuss certain aspects only with their colleagues. In most cases the other party does not object to this and uses the time to its own advantage. This situation requires delicate handling by the interpreter, and successful management depends on the number of interpreters engaged and on whether all parties remain in the same room.

Different aspects of business negotiations

A diverse range of activities can take place during a round of negotiations:

- formal meetings, introductions, welcoming speeches, protocol;
- smaller meetings of groups or even one-on-one meetings at various levels of formality;
- discussions of main points at issue in contracts or work plans;
- technical group meetings which go into detail over plans or specifications;
- visits to relevant sites or institutions;
- extra-curricular activities such as tourist sightseeing or recreation;
- lunches, dinners and banquets at various levels of formality.

Significant variations in discourse can exist during more formal parts of negotiations, particularly during highly technical working-group discussions.

The complexities of technical concepts/processes/jargon are regarded as one of the most difficult aspects of business interpreting. In fact, the more technical the discussion becomes, often the more relaxed the manner of discourse will be. Most of the participants are specialists, who are not concerned with protocol formalities. Their whole purpose is to convey accurate messages and to get things done by whatever means available, and the interpreters can use all kinds of methods to facilitate communication. They can ask the specialists to explain the concept or jargon in a simple way, to spell it out or write it down, to draw a diagram of a technical process or to write the formula. They can even use dictionaries to find the proper term or meaning. Both sides have the capacity to understand technical processes or jargon if spelt out or presented in the form of a diagram on the board, and interpreters should make use of this advantage to overcome the difficulties of the technical material.

The interpreter and the clients

The relationship between the interpreter and the clients bears careful scrutiny. Interpreters often believe that certain ethical principles need to be modified or applied differently in business settings. Typically they argue that because the interpreter is employed as an in-house interpreter by one party, he/she should become a kind of agent for the client, using his/her skills to provide information which the client would not otherwise obtain.

This close contact, coupled with a corporate culture based on fierce loyalty, creates some difficult ethical situations for the interpreter. Economic dependence puts pressure on the interpreter to work for and on behalf of the client, which can undermine the fundamental role of the interpreter as a facilitator of someone else's communication needs. Furthermore, the ethical principle of impartiality is placed under severe strain, especially as often the interpreter, because of bi-cultural competence, is privy to a great deal more information than either party. Often the interpreter is called upon to provide opinions about the other party, about the sincerity of their offers and the likelihood that they will continue to negotiate. The client sees this as legitimate information for the successful clinching of a deal, and has the same expectations of the interpreter as of any other expert or consultant engaged to help with decision-making. The view that the interpreters should be strictly impartial is often criticized by clients as being unrealistic and impractical. This aspect of the role of the interpreter in business settings has not been sufficiently researched for definitive conclusions to be reached.

Deadlocks and the interpreter

A particular issue of ethics arises when negotiations become difficult or deadlocked. Emotions can run high, with both sides expressing frustration or anger. Many business interpreters in such situations play a mediating role. They interpret in a modified way, becoming more diplomatic in their choice of words in order to soften the atmosphere and enable the negotiations to proceed. In so doing, interpreters are not following the ethical principle of accuracy.

The aim of both parties is to get the project or business moving rather than to hurt each other, while at the same time to gain maximum benefit from the business deal. Frequently they will push forward to a breaking point, and then consider a compromise—so deadlocks are very likely. Straightforward interpreting of anger or rudeness may kill a stage of negotiation, while modified interpreting will provide opportunities for the negotiation to move on and succeed.

In such circumstances, it is not enough simply to regard the interpreter as having inexcusably gone outside their role. Frustration or anger in negotiations may arise precisely out of the dynamics of communication, particularly frustration over perceptions of how one's message is getting through and whether it is being understood. Since rudeness or temporary anger is not conducive to the whole process of doing business, both parties will, in the end, be grateful for the modifying influence of an experienced interpreter.

Clearly the interpreter can exercise a good deal of control, but it must always be guided by the principle of facilitating communication rather than hindering it.

The interpreter as a scapegoat

Another pressure is the practice of making the interpreter a scapegoat for errors of judgement or fact made by one of the parties. It is not uncommon for these errors to be remedied by adducing the interpreter's error, with agreement that the positive consequences outweigh the wounding of the interpreter's pride. Where the interpreter draws a limit to this practice is a matter of professional judgement. From an ethical point of view, the interpreter is again being drawn into the unacceptable role of a protagonist. The interpreter may decide to withdraw, sometimes with disastrous results for the client, or may put up with this behaviour for a time but make it clear to the client (outside the interpreting interaction) that other such occurrences will not be tolerated. Both approaches have serious consequences for future employment by that firm. It is generally accepted that the interpreter, in any situation, should not be the cause of the breakdown of communication but a facilitator of such communication.

A similar issue arises when clarification seems required but is not appreciated for reasons of politics, company secrets or technical know-how. Speakers may deliberately deliver ambiguous messages. For instance, in some countries any negative comments on the political system are not tolerated, while comments on other systems are. A businessman may say that difficulties being experienced are related to 'our system'; by the ambiguous use of the word 'system', he is referring obliquely to the political system, but does not expect the interpreter to seek clarification. If the interpreter does not understand this context and seeks clarification, an embarrassing situation may result.

Surviving dinners and banquets

In the past, interpreters often sat behind the main host and guest at dinners and interpreted whatever they said about business or about how delicious the food was. Fortunately, it is not the case any more. The interpreter is now given a seat at the dinner table.

In some countries, seating at dinner is subject to detailed protocol, but almost always the interpreter is included, to ensure communication between the heads of delegations. A knowledge of such protocol is essential for the interpreter, who can enjoy dinner as long as he/she can maintain communication between the two parties.

Participation at dinner demands quick responses in order not to be caught out. Although a dinner or banquet may be quite formal, the atmosphere and communication dynamics are often relaxed. Even if an interpreter is ambushed by a sudden request to interpret while his/her mouth is full, the atmosphere is usually such that the interpreter can use his/her body language to secure a little time, then begin interpreting in an unhurried manner. Interpreters should be able to enjoy dinners, though at so-called 'working' dinners or lunches, they may not be able to eat anything at all.

In summary, interpreting in business settings provides challenges in terms of the nature of the interactions, assumptions made about the interpreter's role, the environment both physical and cultural, and the relationships created by working in a team or by being regarded as an instrument of the client.

10 Speech Pathology

Speech pathology or *speech therapy* encompasses a number of areas and concerns. One large area of work is with communication handicaps in children, whether related to developmental and age-specific issues (e.g. stuttering, clarity of speech) or to physiological factors (cleft palate, genetic anomalies). At the other end of the scale it is concerned with communication difficulties caused by age, or by physical ailments that can occur at any age but are very often found among the elderly (particularly as a result of stroke, trauma or other medical condition). Speech therapy is concerned to restore normal communication functions, but its methods of gaining information are also of importance for wider diagnosis of functioning (other mental processes, thought patterns etc.).

Interpreters must be aware of the finely grained way in which language is used in this field, and in particular of the continual diagnostic uses of language in a wide variety of technical situations. As with mental health, diagnosis is based upon a range of verbal, vocal and paralinguistic behaviours that extends far beyond any normal understanding of a message to be passed from one party to another. But unlike mental health, speech therapy has a restricted field of analysis and highly technical instruments for most areas of analysis and diagnosis.

The bulk of speech therapy work deals with clear deviations from natural language use. Stuttering, slurring, unorthodox pronunciation patterns and confusion in syntax are elements that, in most cases, are apparent to other native speakers; in fact recognition tends to be instant, often with immediate stigmatization. Usually a native speaker can immediately detect the difference between such speech phenomena (generally defined as *speech impediments*) and other traits such as dialect, accent etc. Speech therapy in its diagnostic work is largely concerned with the detailed description of these deviations from norms of speech performance.

If speech therapist and subject do not share a language, it may be difficult for the therapist to be certain if particular linguistic behaviour demonstrates speech impediment, for example whether the subject is stuttering or slurring, or to what degree. If you are not a speaker of, say, Arabic or Chinese, how could you be sure whether a speaker of those languages was stuttering or slurring their words?

The demands on the interpreter are in may ways similar to those in mental health: to render into the other language what can be rendered, and to accurately describe what can't (for example, many of the utterances of stroke patients). It is important that the interpreter not misunderstand their role. In describing the subject's speech, they are not being asked to change professional roles with the speech therapist. The therapist's task is to home in on the features described, invoking patterned variations in performance to test situations in which such impediments do or do not become apparent, more pronounced or less noticeable. This will often closely involve the interpreter in giving responses to particular speech patterns, though the therapist may be able to proceed alone after gaining familiarity with the sounds and their systematic repetition and variation.

Tests for syntactic comprehension

After strokes or other traumas, there is often an additional concern to examine the *syntactic abilities* of the patient in order to test wider mental functions or other aspects of the patient's condition, usually for possible brain damage. This area of increasing involvement by linguists reflects the fundamental role that language plays in thought processes, the prime role of syntax, and the use of linguistic phenomena as a privileged site for their investigation. From a standard textbook in this field, *Disorders of Syntactic Comprehension* (Caplan and Hildebrandt, 1988), we can see that much of the syntactic testing here covers aspects considered to be universals in language. Thus subjects might be asked to discriminate meanings from pictures presented or from stories read to them:

Mary has melted the chocolate
Mary has the melted chocolate (129)

or in specific syntactic-comprehension tests of the form:

The bear that kissed the donkey patted the goat (173)

Patrick was believed by Joe to be eating
Patrick appears to a friend of Joe's to be eating (154)

Such items are usually straightforward (even if they can become increasingly complex) and present only normal issues of accurate translation. But a particular item may be ambiguous in translation: in some languages, for example, tenses are indicated quite differently to English (so that a back-translation may ambiguously give past, present or future variants as equally likely without further markers). The interpreter should alert the therapist to such problems with tense, syntax or semantics. Another problem is that in some languages the number of 'clues' hidden in the text (for example, in number/gender agreements or case endings) can render such items more or less difficult than in English.

More systematic complexities for the interpreters arise from other tests, even of the most informal kind. Almost every doctor who wants to initially test mental functioning will have a large range of simple questions. Most present no problems for interpreters, but those of this kind do:

Here are two words—'frog' and 'Friday'—what do they have in common?

A straight translation of 'frog' and 'Friday' into any other language will miss the point entirely. The doctor is testing whether the patient can grasp easily understood phonological similarities. In another language, quite different items will probably be needed to realize a similar outcome. The interpreter must be alert to this to properly perform the task, and must proceed in close interaction with the therapist.

Some other informal or formal test items use particular *linguistic ambiguities* to test comprehension, as in the case of homonyms or homophones:

> The light hurts my eyes.
> A light jacket is heavy enough for spring. (Gough, 1975: 34)

This sentence pair tests syntactic comprehension of two homonyms, but it is a homonym in English only; in other languages the two expressions for 'light' are unlikely to be homonyms. If the ambiguity embedded in English is important for this test, a quite different item might need to be constructed in the other language. Thus interpreters require specific knowledge of the purpose of particular test items. Changes from such items, if warranted, must be made through the closest interaction between interpreter and therapist, so as to retain the purposes of the original test. It may be difficult or even impossible to create on-the-spot replacement items. The translation of psychological tests of this kind in fact constitutes a specialized field of translation, with an attendant literature on the validity of psychological testing across cultures (Paradis, 1987; Nespoulos and Villiard, 1990).

Other examples abound in the literature: the use of rhyme (e.g. in simple nursery rhyme recognition) contains language-specific features, as do tests involving idioms such as Kingdon-Ward's delightful tests for recognizing mistakes in proverbs:

> Every frog has his day
> A friend in speed is a friend indeed
> The surly bird catches the worm
> Worst come worst served (Kingdon-Ward, 1969: 124)

Here, the correct words rhyme with the incorrect (!) ones. Quite different items will need to be used in other languages.

Similarly, space-filling or cloze exercises need not of themselves be difficult to render into other languages, but may be so if they are looking for specific syntactic structures or are not sensitive to possible syntactic differences in other languages.

Treatment of aphasia

A very significant area of work is with cases of aphasia—distorted communication arising from brain damage, usually trauma or stroke. An extensive literature on this subject is available, and the distinctive patterns of communication of patients have been documented in great detail (Goodglass and Kaplan, 1972; Lecours *et al.*, 1983; Caplan, 1987; Crystal, 1987; Howard and Franklin, 1988). The various forms of aphasia are associated with quite different discourse styles. The literature has identified several distinct kinds of aphasia, etiologically related to different regions of brain damage.

In *Broca's aphasia*, patients' discourse lacks most significant grammatical markers. Here is a typical example (Goodglass and Kaplan, 1972, quoted in Shanks, 1983), from a test where a patient is asked to describe a picture. In the picture of a kitchen, the mother is standing absent-mindedly while her sink overflows; behind her, two children are stealing cookies from the cookie jar on the shelf, but the son who has climbed on a stool to get to the jar is now teetering on the stool:

> Mother's—ah—washin' dishes—but fauza [faucet]—and ova [over]—flowin. Boy—stool—and fall. Cookies—and sister—and mother—day-dreaming. (115)

The interpreter is confronted with a host of issues here: elisions, incomplete words and phrases, no syntactic connection except 'and'. The exactness of this discourse needs to be conveyed—the patient is attempting to identify objects, events, relations, often using single words but attempting to convey what the picture is showing. The therapist needs to know exactly their style of communication.

In cases of *Wernicke's aphasia*, the discourse style is radically different as a patient attempts to describe the same picture:

> Well, I would say that boy is falling off that fence—dangerous. He got hurt and the girl, too, falling off that hanger, and seen some cookies there and coffee's going to fall down also. That's about all I can see in

> that picture there and here the girl is caught in the wet place here, doesn't realize that wet. The water is wetting from the–is flowing over the catch and she's washing–not paying attention to danger there. (116)

Here, the discourse is seemingly fluent, with much better formed sentences than in the previous example, but the description is characterized by vagueness and inaccuracies and a general sense of actual events *not* being described and important relations not understood. The interpreter must convey both the fluency and the redundant and inaccurate information provided.

Even greater vagueness characterizes cases of *Anomic aphasia*:

> Well, it's the–I know what it is, too, and I just can't–ah–well, they're getting ah–this thing here is the think–come–the–ah–I hate to say this, ah, but, I, I–ah–there's something over there–another house, no, that's not a house, I thought it was, but, but this is in–ah–it's–I know what it is. (117)

Unlike Broca's aphasia, key words are omitted almost entirely, there is almost no information and the patient is highly conscious of his/her own difficulties, editorializing on the task at hand and continually facing their lack of comprehension. The task for the interpreter is to convey streams of discourse with almost no actual description but empty lead-in phrases etc. Such nearly incoherent discourse does create significant problems for interpreters, almost as streams of 'nonsense' may do in mental health settings, yet it is crucial to convey precisely the hesitations, vagueness, back-tracking, inconclusiveness.

Other, much rarer, identified aphasias include the somewhat controversially named *jargon aphasia*, where discourse includes many nonsense words, neologisms and complex but empty discourse markers; and *global aphasia* where there is almost total breakdown of both receiving and producing discourse, the patient being able to produce little more than single, repetitive words and phrases.

Clearly, the content of the discourse and its style is crucial to diagnosis, making heavy demands of the interpreter who must be attentive to every nuance in the patient's style of expression. Again, the interpreter may find that there are limits to what can be rendered in the other language, and may need to describe features that can't be rendered. This is a specific requirement of speech pathology interpreting but can also occur in a number of other settings.

Batteries of diagnostic and therapeutic exercises have been developed to test various aspects of *syntactic and semantic performance*. After the identification of categories of aphasia and extent of communication skills, the interpreter will be involved in more fine-grained analysis of the patient's capacities, and an often lengthy therapeutic process of extending the patient's communicative capacity. In cases of formal language evaluation (Albert, 1981) there is generally a progression of language tasks set:

- repetition of single words, phrases;
- passive subject–object order;
- possessive;
- with/to agency;
- prepositions of time and place.

In all of this work, care must be taken to ensure that identified speech from a patient speaking a language not known to the therapist is interpreted in the light of specific features as requested. There are clear linguistic differences between languages in such aspects as use and appropriateness of the passive, and the syntactic features of prepositional and inflected languages etc. The closest working together of therapist and interpreter is called for, so that the object of the test is well understood by the interpreter and suitable adjustments can be made.

A related formal language evaluation can be made of *articulation*: Albert gives examples of the status of critical articulation problems and their use in diagnosis:

> 'chair' pronounced 'tssair'
> 'scissors' pronounced 'klizzors' etc.

Again the interpreter needs to be aware of deviations from the norm in articulation of the other language, and to be constantly feeding back information on this to the therapist.

Even in simple exercises such as *word-repetition* or single word-reading, important deviations by patients give a clue to mental functioning. Howard and Franklin (1988) give examples of single-word repetition mistakes:

'Dorf' (village) repeated as 'Haus' (house)
'Gott' (God) repeated as 'Kirche' (church)

These are simple mis-repeats at the semantic level and present no particular problem for the interpreter. However, mis-repetitions can be made to phonologically similar words:

'port' repeated as 'pork'
'jardinier' (gardener) repeated as 'jardin' (garden)
'lu' (past participle of 'read') repeated as 'lire' (infinitive of 'read')

Here, the interpreter must be able to distinguish phonologically similar from phonologically unrelated mistakes.

Similarly, Marshall and Newcombe (1977) give examples of reading errors where graphically related words have substantial differences in meaning:

'impact' read as 'pact'
'porous' read as 'porcupine'

They hypothesize that reading deviations often result from syllables suggesting other words, which then take over in rendering the particular word:

'allegory' being read as 'lizard' (mediated presumably by alligator)
'gratitude' being read as 'alone' (mediated presumably by solitude)

If the patient is reading in a language not understood by the therapist, the interpreter must be able to describe the patient's responses in a form that will help the therapist formulate conclusions about the patient's reading performance. Several authors have developed taxonomies of error analysis in speech which rely upon the particularities of English pronunciation and syntax (e.g. Kent *et al.*, 1990). Even relatively simple taxonomies show the complexity of the task facing the interpreter. Gruen *et al.* (1990: 167) list the following features of word-generation strategies of brain-injured subjects asked to produce as many word associates as possible of 'S', 'T', 'P' and 'C' given 60 seconds for each letter:

Phonetic similarity

Same initial consonant–vowel syllable	See–Seed
Same initial consonant–consonant cluster	Tree–Trick
Same initial and final consonant with different vowel	Set–Sit
Same initial syllable with different second syllable	Convey–Convince
Homonyms	Two–Too

Semantic similarity

Semantic association	Ship–Sail
Same semantic category	Carrot–Cabbage

Phonetic/Semantic Similarity

Same initial consonant–vowel syllable semantically related	Tot–Toddler

At a more complex level, Locke *et al.* (1973) give examples of dual meanings of words being able to trigger unexpected jumps in discourse. This is a feature of both schizophrenic patients and some aphasic patients, as in this patient statement:

> We gotta get going. We can holler back as soon as they take the first turn and they'll know because there's nothing—they said everything is packed right walls an all we got to do is take the sandwiches out and put the glasses. Many years ago I had them tested. (88)

This shift rests on the dual meaning of the word 'glasses'. For the interpreter relating such a story, it is unlikely that a word with a double meaning in the patient's language has the same double meaning in the therapist's language. Again, co-operation between interpreter and therapist is crucial. The therapist will note such shifts in discourse, but the interpreter must be able to identify the linguistic feature that triggered the shift. Such shifts and triggering can occur at the simplest level, as when a patient was asked to spell the name of a town:

> Oysterville. How do you spell that? O. I'm not quite sure on that. Y. Y–e–s–t–e–r–d–a–y. (89)

The 'y' sound triggers another word, which is then spelt.

The question arises of the appropriateness of certain tests in cross-cultural settings. In the technical literature on aphasia, it is striking how universal aspects of aphasia are, and how language testing (calibrated technically for syntactic and idiomatic features of each language) reveals remarkably similar outcomes across cultures (Nespoulos and Villiard, 1990). There has also been a substantial amount of work done on aphasia in bilinguals, an area of interest to linguistics as it provides clues as to dominance of language and relations between languages.

While various relations are found between languages during aphasia, the emerging consensus in the literature appears to be that in the majority of aphasia cases both languages tend to be affected in similar ways (Duffy, 1972; Paradis, 1987; de Santi *et al.*, 1990). In a now classic description, Duffy pointed to an earlier view that one's native tongue is less affected by aphasia, with patients (or others) sometimes claiming that the patient is still able to speak fluently in a foreign language:

> Misinterpretation often arises in a clinical situation when the examiner is unfamiliar with the second language. If the examination is done by someone familiar with the other language, or when the family is asked to interpret for the patient, the 'foreign language' often turns out to be jargon. (Duffy, 1972: 228)

This may indeed be the one case where having the family interpret is a useful short-cut!

The work of Paradis is important in that he and his colleagues have developed an extensive range of bilingual aphasia tests, which are a resource for both therapists and interpreters. Interestingly, Paradis also advocates sensitivity to language differences and encourages initiatives to vary the tests as appropriate to different languages and their syntax. In English, for example, passive constructions provide greater difficulties than nominal propositions for aphasia patients. But in languages where the passive 'is too artificial, too simple, or nonexistent', Paradis advocates recourse to other structural features, such as changing SVO (subject–verb–object) order, or other syntactic variation. Such initiative must come through team-work between therapist and interpreter.

From these examples, it will be clear that the interpreter must be capable of both rendering linguistic data and describing those features that are not renderable, in order to ensure that the judgements made of speech phenomena accord with the norms of the patient's language. This can involve the interpreter in a very complex relationship with the therapist and the whole testing procedure, and be a most rewarding area of practice.

In summary, in the field of speech pathology, interpreters must be highly conscious of:

- the purposes of the interview/test;
- the nature of any tests and the details of language and tasks involved;
- the often unexpected ways in which aspects of language (phonological, syntactic, semantic) are 'embedded' in material given to subjects.

Texts will often need to be appropriately modified and rendered, not merely translated, into the other language. This necessitates a particularly close working relationship between interpreter and speech pathologist/therapist. Interpreters must often engage in *describing* aspects of a subject's speech or vocal reactions. They need to understand when they are interpreting, when they are giving descriptions of another speaker as any native speaker would (e.g. if a person is stuttering), and when they are describing a particular vocal or verbal aspect to complete their interpreting.

Bibliography

Albert, Martin L. (1981), *Clinical Aspects of Dysphasia*, Vienna, Springer Verlag.
Altman, H. Janet (1987), *Teaching Interpreting: Study and Practice*, London, Centre for Information on Language Teaching and Research.
Anderson, R. Bruce W. (1976), 'Perspectives on the role of the interpreter', in Richard Brislin (ed.), *Translation: Applications and Research*, New York, Gardner.
— (1978), 'Interpreter roles and interpreter situations' in Gerver and Sinaiko [below]
Arjona, Etilvia (1983), 'Language planning in the judicial system: a look at the implementation of the U.S. Court Interpreters Act', *Language Planning Newsletter*, vol. 9, no. 1, February, Honolulu, East-West Centre.
Australia, Attorney-General's Department (1991), *Access to Interpreters in the Australian Legal System*, Canberra, Australian Government Publishing Service.
Australia, Department of Education, Joseph Lo Bianco (1987), *A National Policy on Languages*, Canberra, Australian Government Publishing Service.
Australia, National Accreditation Authority for Translators and Interpreters (NAATI) (1978), *Levels of Accreditation for Translators and Interpreters*, Canberra, Australian Government Publishing Service.
Australian Law Reform Commission (1991), *Discussion Paper No. 48: Multiculturalism: Criminal Law*, Canberra, Australian Government Publishing Service.

Berk-Seligson, Susan (1990), *The Bilingual Courtroom: Court Interpreters in the Judicial Process*, University of Chicago Press.

Bird, Greta (ed.) (1991), *Law in a Multicultural Australia*, Melbourne, National Centre for Cross-Cultural Studies in Law, Monash University.

Blewett, Jill (1987), 'Interpreting and translating in Australia: a celebration of ten years', *The Linguist*, vol. 27, no. 3, Summer 1988 (paper presented to the 8th World Congress of Applied Linguistics, Sydney, August 1987).

Bungay, S. (1985), 'Horse dealing in the U.K.', in *German in the U.K.*, London, Centre for Information on Language Teaching.

Byrne, D. and J. Haydon (1991), *Cross on Evidence*, Sydney, Butterworths.

Campbell, S. and M. D'Argaville (1992), 'Some case studies' in A. Pauwels (ed.) *Cross-Cultural Communication in Legal Settings*, Melbourne, Language and Society Centre, Monash University.

Caplan, David (1987), *Neurolinguistic and Linguistic Aphasiology: An Introduction*, Cambridge University Press.

Caplan, David and Nancy Hildebrandt (1988), *Disorders of Syntactic Comprehension*, Cambridge Mass., MIT Press.

Casement, Patrick (1985), *On Learning from a Patient*, London, Tavistock Institute.

Conley, John M. and William M. O'Barr (1990), *Rules Versus Relationships: The Ethnography of Legal Discourse*, University of Chicago Press.

Corsellis, Anne (1988), 'The community interpreter project', *The Linguist*, vol. 27, no. 1, Winter.

Crystal, David (1987), *Clinical Linguistics*, London, Edward Arnold.

Danet, B. and B. Bogoch (1980), 'Fixed fight or free for all? An empirical study of combativeness in the adversary system of justice', *British Journal of Law and Society*, vol. 7.

D'Argaville, M. (1991), *Cross-Cultural Communication Issues and Solutions in the Delivery of Legal Services*, Melbourne, Centre for Community Languages in the Professions, Monash University.

de Santi, Susan *et al.* (1990), 'Discourse abilities and deficits in multilingual dementia', in Yves Joanette and Hiram B. Brownell (eds), *Discourse Ability and Brain Damage*, New York, Springer Verlag.

Dollerup, Cay and Anne Loddegaard (eds) (1992), *Teaching Translation and Interpreting*, Amsterdam, John Benjamins.

Driesen, Christiane-Jacqueline (1988), 'The interpreter's job: a blow-by-blow account', in C.Picken (ed.), *ITI Conference 2: Translators and Interpreters Mean Business* London, Association of Special Libraries and Information Bureaux.

Duffy, Robert J. (1972), 'Aphasia in adults', in Alan J. Western (ed.), *Communication Disorders: An Appraisal*, Springfield, Charles C. Thomas.

Dunstan, R. (1980), 'Contexts for coercion: analyzing properties of courtroom "questions"', *British Journal of Law and Society* vol. 7.

Feldweg, E. (1989), 'The significance of understanding in the process of interpreting', in L. Gran and J. Dodds (eds), *The Theoretical and Practical Aspects of Teaching Conference Interpreting*, Udine, Campanotto.

Fromkin, V. *et al.* (eds) (1990), *An Introduction to Language*, 2nd edn, Sydney, Holt, Rinehart and Winston.

Gentile, A. (1991), 'Working with professional interpreters', in A. Pauwels (ed.), *Cross-Cultural Communication in Medical Encounters*, Melbourne, Centre for Community Languages in the Professions, Monash University.

Gerver, David and H. Wallace Sinaiko (eds) (1978), *Language Interpretation and Communication*, New York, Plenum Press.

Getzels, J. W. (1958), 'Administration as a social process', in Halpin, A. W. (ed.), *Amininstrative Theory in Education*, Chicago, University of Chicago.

Goodglass, Harold and Edith Kaplan (1972), *The Assessment of Aphasia and Related Disorders*, Philadelphia, Lea & Febiger.

Gough, Philip P. (1975), 'The structure of the language', in Dane D. Drake and Margaret B. Rawson, *Reading, Perception and Language*, Baltimore, York Press.

Gruen, Andrew K. *et al.* (1990), 'Word fluency generational skills of head-injured patients in an acute trauma centre', *Journal of Communication Disorders*, vol. 23.

Halliday, M. A. K. (1981), *Explorations in the Functions of Language*, London, Edward Arnold.

Harris B. and B. Sherwood (1978), 'Translating as an innate skill', in D. Gerver and W. Sinaiko (eds), *Language, Interpretation and Communication*, New York, Plenum.

Heath, Shirley Brice and Frederick Mandabach (1983), 'Language status descisions and the law in the United States', in J. Cobarrubias and J. Fishman (eds), *Progress in Language Planning*, Berlin, Walter de Gruyter.

Herbert, Jean (1978), 'How conference interpreting grew', in Gerver and Sinaiko [above].

Hermes, Klaus (1987), Professionalism and Ethics in Interpreting and Translating (unpublished paper obtained from the author).

Howard, David and Sue Franklin (1988), *Missing the Meaning?*, Cambridge Mass., MIT Press.

Kent, Raymond C. *et al.* (1990), 'Impairment of speech intelligibility in men with amyotrophic lateral sclerosis', *Journal of Speech and hearing Disorders*, vol. 55, November.

Kingdon-Ward, Winifred (1969), *Helping the Stroke Patient to Speak*, London, Churchill.

KPMG Peat Marwick Management Consultants (1990), *Language Services Report*, Sydney, Department of Immigration, Local Government and Ethnic Affairs.

Lando, John (n.d.), *Interpreting for the Speech Pathologist: A Manual for Use with Italian Patients*, Melbourne, Central Health Interpreter Service.

Lang, Ranier (1978), 'Behavioural aspects of liaison interpreters in Papua New Guinea: some preliminary observations', in Gerver and Sinaiko [above].

Larson, Mildred (1984), *Meaning-Based Translation: A Guide to Cross-Language Equivalence*, London, Unversity of America Press.

Laster, Kathy (1990), 'Legal interpreters: conduits to social justice?', *Journal of Intercultural Studies*, vol. 11, no. 1.

Laster, Kathy and Taylor, Veronica (1994), *Interpreters and the Legal System*, Sydney, Federation Press.

Lecours, Andra Roch, Francoise L'hermitte and Bonnie Bryans (1983), *Aphasiology*, Eastbourne, Balliere Tindall.

Locke, Simeon, David Caplan and Lucia Keller (1973), *A Study in Neurolinguistics*, Springfield, Charles C. Thomas.

Marshall, John C. and Freda Newcombe (1977), 'Variability and constraint in acquired dyslexia', in Haiganoosh Whitaker and Harry A. Whitaker (eds), *Studies in Neurolinguistics*, vol. 3, New York, Academic Press.

Munkman, John H. (1951), *The Technique of Advocacy*, London, Stevens (reprinted 1986, Sweet & Maxwell, London).

Nespoulos, Jean-Luc and Pierre Villiard (1990), *Morphology, Phonology and Aphasia*, New York, Springer Verlag.

O'Barr, William M. (1982), *Linguistic Evidence: Language, Power and Strategy in the Courtroom*, New York, Academic Press.

Ozolins, Uldis (1991), *Interpreting Translating and Language Policy*, Melbourne, National Languages Institute of Australia.

Paradis, Michel (1987), *The Assessment of Bilingual Aphasia*, Hillsdale, Lawrence Erlbaum Associates.

Paralleles: Cahiers de l'Ecole de Traduction et d'Interprétation, University of Geneva.

Picken, Catriona (ed.) (1989), *ITI Conference Proceedings 3*, London, Association of Special Libraries and Information Bureaux.

Roberts-Smith, J. (1990), 'Interpreters and the Law', in Frey *et al.* (eds), *Working with Interpreters*, Canberra, National Accreditation Authority for Translators and Interpreters.

Robinson, Ludmilla (1994), *Handbook for Legal Interpreters*, Sydney, Law Book Company.

Roland, Ruth (1982), *Translating World Affairs*, Jefferson, McFarland & Co.

Rosenbaum, Bent (1987), 'The discourse of psychosis and the process of listening', in Iris M. Zavala, Myriam Diaz-Diocareti and Tuen A. Van Dijk, *Approaches to Discourse, Poetics and Psychiatry*, Amsterdam, John Benjamins.

Rosenbaum, Bent and Harly Sonne (1986), *The Language of Psychosis*, New York, New York University Press.

Rozan, Jean-François (1956), *La Prise de notes en interprétation consécutive*, Geneva, Libraire de l'Université.

Sales, Bruce Dennis (1977), *The Criminal Justice System*, New York, Plenum Press.

Schweda-Nicholson, Nancy (1992), 'The provision of interpretation services for lesser-used languages in the United States', *Language Problems and Language Planning*, vol. 16, no. 1.

S.G.S. Associates (Education) Ltd (1979), *Translating and Interpreting*, London, Career and Occupational Information.

Shackman, Jane (1984), *The Right to be Understood*, Cambridge Mass., National Extension College.

Shanks, Susan J. (1983), *Nursing and the Management of Adult Communication Disorders*, San Diego, College Hill Press.

Simon, Paul (1980), *The Tongue-Tied American: Confronting the Foreign Language Crisis*, New York, Continuum.

Sullivan, Harry Stack (1954), *The Psychiatric Interview*, New York, W. W. Norton

Taylor, C. (1989), 'Textual memory and the teaching of consecutive interpretation', in L. Gran and J. Dodds (eds), *The Theoretical and Practical Aspects of Teaching Conference Interpreting*, Udine, Campanotto.

Tebble Helen (1991), 'Towards a theory of interpreting', in Hellander, P. (ed.), *CITEAA XIII Proceedings*, Conference of the Interpreter and Translator Educators' Association of Australia, Adelaide, South Australian College of Advanced Education.

Tebble Helen (1993), 'A discourse model for dialogue interpreting', in *AUSIT Proceedings of the First Practitioners' Seminar*, Canberra, National Australian Association of Translators and Interpreters.

Thomas, Noel and Richard Towell (1985), *Interpreting as a Language Teaching Technique*, London, Centre for Information on Language Teaching and Research.

Thompson, John R. (1987), *The Process of Psychotherapy*, Lanham, University Press of America.
Ton-That, Q. D. (1991), 'Legal interpreting: an interpreter's view', paper presented at XIV CITEA (Conference of Interpreter Translator Educators of Australia), Melbourne.
Ton-That, Q. D. (1992), 'Legal interpreting' in A. Pauwels (ed.), *Cross-Cultural Communication in Legal Settings*, Melbourne, Language and Society Centre, Monash University.
Toury, Gideon (1984), 'Natural translation and the making of a native translator', *Proceedings of 7th AILA (International Association for Applied Linguistics) Congress*, PLACE TO COME.
United States, Congress, Senate, Committee on the Judiciary, Subcommittee on the Constitution (1986), *Court Interpreters Improvement Act of 1984: Hearing Before the Committee*, Washington D.C., Serial J-99-88.
Weber, Wilhelm K. (1984), *Training Translators and Conference Interpreters*, Orlando, Harcourt Brace Jovanovich.
White, P.T. (1955), 'The interpreter: linguist plus diplomat', *New York Times Magazine*, 6 November.
Willis, J. and Sallman (1984), *Criminal Justice in Australia*, Melbourne, Oxford University Press.
Wilss, Wolfram (1982), *The Science of Translation*, Tübingen, Gunter Narr Verlag.
Yoken, C. (1980), *Interpreter Training, USA*, National Academy of Gallaudet College.
Zhong, S. (1984), *A Practical Handbook of Interpretation*, Peking, Chungkuo Tui Wai Fun I Ch'n Pan Kung Ssu, China Foreign Press.
Zhou, Z. (1988), *The Theory and Practice of Interpreting*, Hong Kong, Commercial Press.
Zweig, J. K. (1982), *Ericksonian Approaches to Hypnosis and Psychotherapy*, New York, Brunner/Mozel.

Index

Note: as the overall theme of this book is liaison interpreting, this term is not indexed; see separate headings for fields of work (e.g. 'medical interpreting') or issues (e.g. 'role of interpreter') etc.

Aborigines, 5
accreditation of interpreters, 3, 10, 61, 95
accuracy, 49–50, 101, 122
advocates, interpreters as, 2, 15, 29
AIIC, *see* International Association of Conference Interpreters
ambiguity, deliberate, 123
aphasia, 129–31, 134
Arabic, 5, 59–60, 126
articulation, in speech pathology, 131
asides during interpreting, 21, 36
audience size, 23, 25
Australia, 2, 4, 10, 11, 61, 94

bias in interpreting, 59
bilingual aides, 12, 14
bilingual guides, 14–15
bilingual helpers, 13–15, 31
body language, 51, 112
briefing, 21, 32, 44, 48, 49, 53, 55, 95, 118
Britain, 7, 17

business, interpreting in, 2, 3, 9, 11–12, 18, 38, 41, 61–2, 65, 78, 116–24

Chinese, 126
chuchotage, 26, 117
'client' concept, 36–7
colonialism, 6
communication dynamics, 18, 51–3, 55, 67, 112
communicative therapy, 3, 81–3
community interpreting, 17, 65
conduit, interpreter as, 103, 114
conference interpreting, 2, 3, 7–12, 15, 17, 19, 22–4, 33, 37–8, 65, 71–2, 118–19
confidentiality, 58–9
conflict of interest, 59–60
Congress of Vienna, 7
consecutive interpreting, 7–8, 22–4, 27
contact interpreting, 17, 65
control of interpreting situations, 24, 26, 39, 51–3

counselling, 25, 72, 78
court interpreting, 3, 18, 22, 27, 38, 65, 78, 90–1, 93ff.
cross-examination, 94–6, 105–6, 110–15
cultural factors in interpreting, 19–21, 54–5, 60, 117

debriefing, 44
decoding, 101
demeanour, 78, 80
describing features of communication, 84, 87, 126, 131, 135
diagnosis, 18, 62, 125, 130
dialects, 46–7
dialogue interpreting, 17, 65
diplomacy, interpreting in, 6–8
distortions of communication, 79, 85–7, 89

education, interpreting needs in, 5, 18, 19, 25, 59, 60, 62
emotional factors, 26, 84, 122
English, 12, 48, 90, 127–8
ethical issues, 3, 14, 21, 31, 32, 42, 56–63, 95, 119, 121–3
ethics, code of, 58
ethnic groups and identity, 14, 33, 59
evidence-in-chief, 94–6, 105, 107–10
eye contact, 25, 42

family therapy, 41
Federal Court Interpreters Act, 104
feedback loop, 35
filter, interpreter as, 49
first person/third person in interpreting, 26, 42, 88
fluency, 47
forensic aspects, 3, 77
French, 5, 7, 23

Gaio v. R, 103, 105
gender issues, 20, 59
German/Germany, 11, 23
government involvement in interpreting, 10, 64
Gradidge v. Grace Brothers Pty Ltd, 95, 104

group therapy, 18

hearsay, 103, 108

idiomatic language, 50
immigrants, 1, 2, 9–13
impartiality, 58, 60, 121–2
indigenous populations, 1, 2, 9–13
industrial issues for interpreters, 3, 10, 69
International Association of Conference Interpreters, 8
interpreting by relatives or friends, 8, 13–14, 134
interrupting while interpreting, 24–6, 45–6, 55, 67, 84, 109, 112
intervening in situations, 34
Italian, 23

language competence, 65
Latin, 5
lawyer/client conferences, 91, 93–5, 105–6
legal interpreting, 1–4, 10–11, 18, 26, 43, 48–9, 62, 89–115
legal language, 95ff., 105ff., 115
legal submission, 98–9
lingua franca, 5
'linguistically present' doctrine, 102, 104, 114
listening skills, 44–5, 55

medical interpreting, 1, 2, 18, 20, 24, 41, 48, 59, 60, 62–3, 90
memory, 28–9, 45, 67–8, 84, 88
mental health interpreting, 3, 26–7, 38, 77, 79–89, 105, 126
minorities, 2, 13, 16
minority language, 14–15

negotiations, 72, 119–22
neologisms, 86–7
note-taking, 26–8, 39, 67–8, 84
Nuremberg war trials, 8

pauses, 83–4

143

physical environment of interpreting, 18, 23, 29, 31, 79, 116–17
physical presence of interpreter, 17–18, 32–3, 40
police interpreting, 18, 20, 43, 59, 60, 90–3, 106
professional development, 10, 38, 56–9, 69
professional negligence, 61
professional socialization, 64–73
psychiatric interview, 79–80
psychosis, language of, 86–7

R v. Lee Kun, 102
racism, 13
redundancy in speech, 67
re-examination of a witness, 96, 98, 106
refugees, 20
register, 47–50, 55, 66
religions, 5, 7
right to silence, 91
role of interpreters, 1–3, 6, 11–15, 23, 29, 30–40, 72–3, 89, 100–5, 117, 121–4, 126; educational role, 73
role reciprocal, 30, 32

Scandinavia, 2, 10, 85
scapegoat, interpreter as, 122–3
sentencing, 99–100
simultaneous interpreting, 1, 22, 26, 84, 88
slips of the tongue, 87
social status differentials, 18, 20–1, 33–4
Spanish, 59–60, 112
spatial arrangements, 18, 67
speech impediments, 126
speech pathology/speech therapy, 3, 77, 125–35
status of message, 77–8
stress in interpreting, 29
strokes, 125–9
subtitling, 40
syntactic comprehension, 126–9

taping of interviews, 91–2
teamwork in interpreting, 118–19, 124
three-cornered interpreting, 17, 52–3, 65
tourism, 12, 14
trade/traders, 5–6, 41
training of interpreters, 2–4, 8, 50, 56, 69–72
translation, 7, 28, 30, 39–40; sight translation, 39–40, 91
turn-taking, 25, 35–6, 84, 112–14

United States, 2, 7, 10, 104

Versailles peace talks, 7
vocal communication, 80, 84, 87–8, 112, 135

warnings, interpreting of, 91
welfare interpreting, 1–2, 10, 62
World War I, 7
World War II, 3, 8–9